The HEALING
JOURNEY

ALSO BY THOM GARDNER

Healing the Wounded Heart

AVAILABLE FROM DESTINY IMAGE PUBLISHERS

The HEALING JOURNEY

An Interactive Guide to Spiritual Wholeness

THOM GARDNER

DESTINY IMAGE® PUBLISHERS, INC.

P.O. Box 310, Shippensburg, PA 17257-0310

"Speaking to the Purposes of God for This Generation and for the Generations to Come."

This book and all other Destiny Image, Revival Press, MercyPlace, Fresh Bread, Destiny Image Fiction, and Treasure House books are available at Christian bookstores and distributors worldwide.

For a U.S. bookstore nearest you, call **1-800-722-6774**.

For more information on foreign distributors, call **717-532-3040**.

Reach us on the Internet: **www.destinyimage.com**.

Trade Paper ISBN 13: 978-0-7684-3230-5
Hard Cover ISBN 13: 978-0-7684-3414-9
Large Print ISBN 13: 978-0-7684-3415-6
Ebook ISBN 13: 978-0-7684-9066-4

For Worldwide Distribution, Printed in the U.S.A.

1 2 3 4 5 6 7 8 9 10 11 / 13 12 11 10

CONTENTS

PROLOGUE

Greetings in the name of the Lord Jesus Christ!

Welcome to your *Healing Journey*. You are about to embark on an intentional season of healing the wounds of your heart. As you heal, obstacles to intimacy with God will be removed. You will find that not only will you receive healing, but you will also experience a real deepening of your relationship with the Lord.

The purpose for healing is not just the reduction of the emotional pain in your life or solving the issues and struggles you face; it is coming into a place of unhindered intimacy with God that will release you into your destiny. Healing is but another step in our becoming better disciples of Jesus Christ. As you heal, you will encounter the Lord face to face, becoming a friend of God (see Exod. 33:11). You will experience a soul that prospers (see 3 John 2) and begin to live the life the Father has dreamed for you.

There are several different parts to this interactive guide book. Part One consists of a chapter called Safe to Heal. In this chapter you will learn how to find a safe place in the your heart in which to meet with Jesus in an interactive and personal way. This will provide the venue for further healing and meditation. You will also find helpful step-by-step instructions to get you started on your interactive journey. It will help you experience the Lord's presence in life-changing ways as you continue in the personal healing Word of God journaling and meditation in the Scriptures.

Part Two forms the main part of the Journal. It holds seven weeks of scriptural focus for healing and growth organized on a topical basis. Each day you will be invited to meditate and interact with a verse or two of scripture and enter your responses on the page. It is also important to visit the Weekly Summary at the end of Section Two to capture the truths that have been revealed to you.

In Part Three you will be invited to continue the journey for as long as you like, hopefully a lifetime. You will be provided with a blank format similar to Part Two but in this case you will choose a Scripture from among the topical list of Scripture we provide in this book or any other topical list you choose. Our goal is to encourage you to continue using the Scriptures as an interactive source of inspiration in which you experience the breath and presence of God in a transforming way.

Part Four is a simple and useful tool that allows you to capture anxious thoughts—thoughts that do not agree with what God says about you. There is great value in actually writing down our anxious thoughts and taking them captive in Christ through his words and presence.

Finally, the Appendix provides Mark Virkler's four keys to hearing the voice of God. This has been an encouragement and resource to me personally for many years. I have provided these keys here with Dr. Virkler's permission as a treasure for your continued spiritual growth.

May the Lord embrace you with His presence as you embark on this *Healing Journey!*

INTRODUCTION

BEGINNING YOUR HEALING JOURNEY

IN the following pages, you will find multiple tools to enhance your healing experience and grow closer to the Lord who has drawn you into this season. He loves you and has extended a personal invitation to you to come into His presence to find rest and peace. Your healing was His idea.

It is important to be consistent in your *Healing Journey*. To that end, you will find a 49-day devotional that will lead you to find personal Truth through interacting with the Scriptures. These daily encounters have intentionally been made brief so that you will find it easier to be consistent in your healing devotional time. You will also find a weekly summary at the end of each topical section so that you can discover how much you have grown in the knowledge of God and the healing of your heart.

The Bible is a succession of thousands of pictures through which we may see the Father's heart. In this devotional, you will be invited to *see* and experience the Scriptures in a personal way. Instead of reading for understanding, you will experience Truth for transformation.

The Lord continues to speak to us in these thousands of pictures through Scripture. The Bible tells us, *"The heavens are telling of the glory of God; and their expanse is declaring the work of His hands. Day to day pours forth speech, and night to night reveals knowledge"* (Ps. 19:1-2). The Word of God in the Scriptures is alive with fresh revelation and personal application for our healing.

Dr. Mark Virkler is a prolific writer in the area of hearing God's voice and has offered much teaching and a simple approach to tuning into the heart of God. Dr. Virkler says, "God's voice and God's visions come to us as spontaneous thoughts and spontaneous pictures which light upon us, especially when we are in God's presence." We must learn to open our hearts to the fresh oil being squeezed out of the Word of God as we meditate upon it and allow our hearts to *see* it. Note that I have included Dr. Virkler's instructions for hearing the voice of God at the end of this book, beginning on page 265. It may be helpful to read these four steps before you begin the Day 1 meditation. These steps are a general guideline for hearing God's voice and will be useful for any further journaling you may want to do on the lined pages supplied at the end of this book.

I also recommend that you keep a separate journal where you may meditate on additional Scriptures. As you meditate on the scriptural texts, I suggest that you use the images that the Lord provides as the setting for hearing from the Lord as you journal.

When we see the Scriptures and experience the presence of God, we find a greater order and peace to continue on the healing journey. Each daily section begins with a verse of Scripture upon which you will meditate.

To meditate in the biblical sense, you will read the verse aloud several times in a soft voice until you can say it with your eyes closed. As you repeat the Scripture, an image will form in your mind. To that end we have chosen healing verses that are rich in visual imagery. Once you can picture the Scripture in your mind, you will be invited to respond to a few questions that will allow you to experience Truth and healing in the personal presence of God. We are asking:

- "What do you see?"

- "What does it say about the heart of God?"

- "What is God speaking to you personally through this verse?"

Note that some people are not as visual as others. In this case we must rephrase our instructions. If you are not given to visual imagery, simply focus on a key word or phrase that stands out to you. As you meditate on that key word or phrase, let your heart consider what that word or phrase means. Construct a mental image of what that word or phrase looks like to you in your own experience.

Here is an example to get us started in scriptural meditation. Read the following text aloud in order to practice biblical meditation.

> *I am the vine, you are the branches; he who abides in Me and I in him, he bears much fruit, for apart from Me you can do nothing* (John 15:5).

Repeat this text a few times until you can say it with your eyes closed. What do you picture in your mind as you repeat the verse? Perhaps the image of a vine laden with fruit fills your mind. You might see the close attachment of the branches and the vine. In any event, the Lord is speaking something to you as you meditate on His Word. Because it is a visual image, it will remain with you—become part of you.

This verse may speak to you of the attachment and faithfulness of the Father toward you. This may then hold a personal word that you are joined to God in a way that allows you to bear fruit that He is producing—that you will remain in Him and He will produce something in you. If you find that the Scripture text for that day is too long, just pick out one clause for meditation.

In each daily section, you will also find a quotation from *Healing the Wounded Heart: Removing Obstacles to Intimacy with God,* which will help you to focus and will support the healing truth of God's Word.[1] Healing is a journey of many steps. Some steps will be sudden, as brilliant and intimate revelation dawns on your heart. Other steps are softer, shorter. At the end of the journey will be the Father's heart. May you be blessed on your journey.

It is vital to your healing journey that you complete one devotional each day. Do not do more than one. This is not a race or a chore to be completed. It is a walk with the personal and intimate presence of the Lord.

At the end of each one of the seven weeks, you are invited to write a short summary of what the Lord has spoken to you each day. This will help you to build healing and revelation line upon line and allow you to see that you are on a clear and steady path to greater intimacy with God. It is no accident that there are seven weeks of seven devotions per week. This daily devotional meditation will bring you a jubilee—a new freedom to follow Jesus.

(A sidenote to Bible students: The scriptural selections we have used are not presented in their entire context but rather excerpted for the deeper-heart truths they represent. It is important when we teach or preach from the Scriptures to consider the historical, literary, and grammatical contexts. We must ask God's intention and the plain meaning of the text. However, there is a deeper context we are seeking here. We want the context of God's character and heart to come to the foreground. For example, in Matthew 28:20, when Jesus says, *"I am with you always, even to the end of the age,"* He is commissioning His followers who will go into the world and encounter difficulties and challenges. There is a deeper heart truth that Christ is with us always.)

I pray and trust that the Lord will bless you as you place your hand in His to begin your *Healing Journey*.

ENDNOTE

1. Thom Gardner, *Healing the Wounded Heart: Removing Obstacles to Intimacy with God* (Shippenburg, PA: Destiny Images Publishers, Inc., 2005).

PART I:

A Safe Place to Heal

SAFE TO HEAL

Then the Lord said, "Behold, there is a place by Me" (Exodus 33:21).

A S we begin a season of healing, it's good to establish a place in our hearts and minds for connecting and communing with the Lord. I find it helpful to find a meeting place—a safe place where the Lord speaks to me through words, images, Scriptures, thoughts, and any other number of ways. You will be invited to go to a safe place in your heart to soak in the Scriptures and truth. This will become a place where it is *safe to heal*.

Your safe place will be a place of meditation where you will close your eyes and allow the Lord to interact with you. It is a place where you listen to Him speaking to your heart and learn to hear His voice.

First, here is a little note about navigating new destinations in your heart and mind. Our imagination is a gift from God. It is a part of us. We folks in the West need to develop our flabby imaginations and learn to meditate on the truth of God as David did. Some of us are so worried about being deluded and deceived by the devil that we put all our creative imagery on the shelf, which is unfortunate.

As we begin this healing journey, we should ask the Lord to make our imagination holy ground purchased by the blood of Christ. We can have the mind and imagination of Christ! (See First Corinthians 2:16.)

THE MEMORY-BASED SAFE PLACE

There are two effective ways to find a safe place to heal: Memory-based and Scripture-based safe places. Either one is more effective than a place of pure imagination because there are fewer distractions. I have also found that safe places without historical reference or scriptural foundation are less real to us. The main issue here is that when we provide a personal and historical frame of reference, the enemy cannot easily corrupt our safe place. He cannot change history even when we remember things in a subjective way. For example, if I recall a safe place by a brook behind my grandfather's house, that place is limited to my personal experience and recollection. If it is merely a product of my imagination that has no basis in truth, then it is open to corruption and other influences that were not a part of that scene. Limiting the safe place to our personal history and frame of reference limits interference from other sources.

A memory-based safe place is just like it sounds: It is from our own memory. This safe place is one we experience in our own previous history. It is important, however, that the place is real and historic and not just imagined. To find such a place, you may just close your eyes and think of a place where you felt very comfortable and secure—a place where you felt quieted. Some folks may recall feeling safe in their grandparents' home or by a stream they fished in as a child. For others, those places are not pleasant or peaceful. One way to find such a safe place is to ask yourself what image comes to mind when you say words to yourself like "peace" or "restful" or "safe."

THE SCRIPTURE-BASED SAFE PLACE

The Scriptures provide an environment with thousands of healing moments and built-in safe places. The best passages are those with ready visual images such as Psalm 23. Through the Scriptures we engage our visual ability in a non-threatening, gentle way. I find that scriptural safe places are very effective and also provide ongoing opportunity for meditation during seasons of healing.

As we read the Scriptures, the Lord frequently brings images to our minds. For example, what might you picture in your mind when you read these words? *"The Lord is my shepherd, I shall not want..."* (Ps. 23:1). Do you have a mental image of a shepherd holding a lamb? You may have even called to mind a picture you saw of Jesus as the Good Shepherd. That image can become a safe place for you to have a conversation with the Shepherd.

Many times we have a favorite Scripture or life verse that has been meaningful to us. There is a reason why those verses are meaningful. Many times they meet a core need or touch some deep place of healing truth. Think for a minute of your own favorite verses. What images do those verses bring to mind?

There are a few guidelines for using this Scripture-based safe place technique:

1. Use short portions of Scripture.

2. Use Scriptures with lots of visual imagery—phrases like "eagles' wings" or "shadow of the Almighty" or those that refer to Christ as a "Shepherd" or God as a "Father."

3. Focus on the lines containing personal interaction with God's presence or character.

4. Use an easy-to-understand Bible version, such as the New Living Translation, the New International Version, the New American Standard Bible, etc. (Note: We are not trying to score theological points; we are bringing the wounded into the images and experience of the Scripture.)

One passage that I frequently visit is Mark 6:30-31 (NIV):

> *The apostles gathered around Jesus and reported to Him all they had done and taught. Then, because so many people were coming and going that they did not even have a chance to eat, He said to them,* **"Come with Me by yourselves to a quiet place and get some rest."**

When I read these verses a few times and then close my eyes, I can almost see Jesus getting into a little fishing boat with His friends and slowly making for some hidden and quiet place. I can hear the water lapping against the shoreline with seagulls flying overhead. I have images of Jesus enjoying time with those with whom He shared so much life, each one feeling as though they are the only one there. The *"quiet place"* to which Jesus invited them was meant for connection and rest. When I visit this place I feel safe and hidden away with Christ. When I visit this place and have come to rest, I sometimes share my heart with the Lord. Sometimes He shares His right back to me.

There are a few other suggestions for safe places. It should be noted that each of us has a different life experience and areas of wounding. Therefore not all Scripture will be appropriate for everyone. For example, if a person was molested by someone as she sat on his knee as a child, then to be "Fondled on the knee" would not be a good thought. There have been times when some folks we ministered to were so wounded that we had to first read a suggested safe verse and ask them how they felt. If that place was not good, then we moved on to another. I suggest you do this as you begin to search for safe places in the Scriptures. Fortunately, we all have thousands of verses from which to choose. You may simply substitute a Scripture from the list of additional topical Scriptures.

Allow the Lord to invite you to the mercy seat in Psalm 91:1-2. Lie down in the green pastures or be led by the still waters of Psalm 23. Perhaps you may find rest as you come to the One whose yoke is light, as mentioned in Matthew 11:28-30, or experience deep rest while leaning against His heart, as in John 13:23.

You may look for themes, such as being carried by the Lord:

> *...in the wilderness where you saw how the Lord your God carried you, just as a man carries his son, in all the way which you have walked until you came to this place* (Deuteronomy 1:31).

Or:

Listen to Me, all you who are left in Israel. I created you and have cared for you since before you were born. I will be your God throughout your lifetime—until your hair is white with age. I made you, and I will care for you. I will carry you along and save you (Isaiah 46:3-4 NLT).

There are Scriptures that bring the image of God as a safe place Himself.

*...God is a **safe hiding place**, a granite safe house for the children of Israel* (Joel 3:16 TM).

*God is good, a **hiding place** in tough times. He recognizes and welcomes anyone looking for help* (Nahum 1:7 TM).

*God is a **safe place** to hide, ready to help when we need Him* (Psalm 46:1 TM).

*For You've been a **safe place** for me, a good place to hide* (Psalm 59:16 TM).

*God's name is a place of protection—good people can run there and be **safe*** (Proverbs 18:10 TM).

Each daily meditation and the additional topical listing of Scriptures offers a choice of verses for meditation. Many of these could also be employed as safe places. Here are two basic guidelines:

1. Read the relevant lines of Scripture several times, then close your eyes and allow images to come to mind. Make a personal connection with the Lord in those images. Allow yourself to feel the physical touch or connection with the Lord.

2. What is being communicated from the heart of the Lord to you? Speak that truth aloud. It may be good to write it down in your

journal or even in this book. Now let's practice establishing safe places.

FINDING A MEMORY-BASED SAFE PLACE

Think about the words *rest, quiet,* or *secure.* Do any of these words bring to mind locations when you were a child? Are there places in your life right now that are safe for you? Here are a few suggestions to find a memory-based safe place.

1. Stop right at this moment and ask the Lord to bring to mind a place from your own personal history that felt safe and secure. Maybe it was the home of your grandparents or in a quiet place under a favorite tree.

2. If the Lord brings such a place to mind, invite Him to express His presence there. Remember, the Lord expresses His presence in a variety of ways. There is no one right way. (I am including a section called "The Sound of Truth" at the end of this section to help you determine what is God and what is not, based on Psalm 19:7-10.)

3. As you make the connection, release any anxious thoughts to the Lord and be open to any thoughts or images He may wish to communicate to you. I suggest you write in your journal anything you sense the Lord bringing to you. We will leave a little space here to do so.

THE SOUND OF TRUTH

We might ask how we can know whether God is the one speaking to us, or if it is our own human thoughts, or even if it is the enemy. The best way to discern what we are hearing is to keep in mind this simple fact: The truth of God reflects the character of God. We can know something is the truth of God's

Word to us by the character and effect of it. Psalm 19:7-10 gives us a good idea of the character of God's truth. In this psalm there are several synonyms for the communication of God: the law, testimony, precepts, commandment, fear, and the judgments of God. We can listen to what we hear and compare it to the sound of truth in this psalm:

> *The law of the Lord is **perfect, restoring the soul**; the testimony of the Lord is **sure, making wise the simple**. The precepts of the Lord are **right, rejoicing the heart**; the commandment of the Lord is **pure, enlightening the eyes**. The fear of the Lord is **clean, enduring forever**; the judgments of the Lord are **true**; they are **righteous altogether**. They are **more desirable than gold**, yes, than much fine gold; sweeter also than honey and the drippings of the honeycomb (Psalm 19:7-10, emphasis added).*

Psalm 19 is a description of God's voice and what He is likely to say to us. It is a description of the Torah, and uses several different words such as *law*, or *testimony*; but for our purpose here, each one is just another way of saying, God's voice has the following qualities.

Perfect, Restoring the Soul

This word for "perfect" is the Hebrew word *tamiym*, which describes a state of wholeness. When God speaks, it is meant to bring wholeness. God does not speak in a way that tears me down but in words that will ultimately lead to my healing and restoration. Yes, God speaks to us to discipline us when we need it. But even those words are tempered with mercy. In His wrath, He always remembers mercy (see Hab. 3:2). God's words to us always draw us back to His bosom. Those words that push us away from His heart are not God's words. The words of God are the words of a perfect Father who has a perfect love for His children. He does not speak to us out of some kind of insecurity nor does He try to manipulate us with threats and fear.

God's voice leads us to restoration or perhaps conversion. He invites us into His heart and presence. It doesn't seem likely that God would invite us by greeting us with a stick. I would sum it up by saying that the words I hear from God are healing words that invite me to greater intimacy with Him.

Sure, Making Wise the Simple

When God speaks, He does so with clarity. *"God is not a God of confusion but of peace..."* (1 Cor. 14:33). If we agree that God leads us through what He says, then what possible purpose would there be for Him to speak with confusion? God speaks in clear and uncluttered language, not shrouded in darkness and mystery.

God will not speak in a way that paralyses me and prevents me from moving toward Him or into His purposes. He speaks in a way that gives me confidence to respond to His voice. Imagine getting an invitation in the mail that doesn't tell you what you are invited to or where. Again, God's desire is that we draw near to Him. He does not play mind games with us. His Word has been compared to a light for us. *"Your word is a lamp to my feet, and a light to my path "* (Ps. 119:105). To be sure, God does not always give us the whole picture or all the details, but He will always lead us to the next step.

God invites us and leads us to Himself. When He speaks to us, His words and meaning are clear and give us confidence to respond to what He says.

Right, Rejoicing the Heart

God's voice has a kind of resonance about it. Anything that the Lord speaks to us has a right ring to it. The word "right" here is the Hebrew word *yashar*, which is a kind of ethical and moral rightness. The literal meaning is *straight.* When God speaks to us, He is leading us in simplicity to what would please Him. It's that kind of feeling we get when we study hard for a spelling test and know that we have the whole list down cold. There is a confidence in what we hear—that it is right.

The Lord's voice leads us in a way that agrees with His nature. He speaks to us in a way that reflects the needs and hearts of other people. God does not compromise Himself or His Word; indeed, He cannot contradict Himself. He is the Lord God, the Creator! He does not change His nature on a whim. He is not intimidated by our opinion of Him. He is completely holy and above our opinions.

There is a resonance in our hearts when God speaks—a feeling of joy that is not dependent on circumstances. When we hear God, the Lord brings us to a place where we are settled and at rest. Our heart rejoices with His heart because we agree with Him that we belong to Him.

Pure, Enlightening the Eyes

When we say that God's voice is pure, we mean that it is obviously free of any impurity, but also, and perhaps more importantly, we are saying that God's voice is free of any mixed motive. God has chosen to love us, and when He tells us that He loves us, He is not leading us on. We need not wait for the other shoe to fall.

The effect of the purity of God's motives and love toward us *helps us to see ourselves as He sees us*. When the Bible uses the phrase "enlightening the eye," it is talking about our mind. When God tells us what He thinks and feels about us, our hearts and attitudes change. We live as the beloved of God, and so we are.

Enduring...True...Righteous...Clean—Giving Me Confidence and Peace

When God speaks to us, He is not interested in the mundane. He does not go through our sock drawer or put on a white glove to see how often we dust. God is an eternal God and speaks to us about eternal things. What He says to us is solid, enduring, eternal, and righteous. There is an unchangeableness about the voice of God.

When God speaks to me, He draws me into the realm of eternity with Him. The psalmist said, *"Forever, O Lord, Your word is settled in heaven. Your faithfulness continues throughout all generations; You established the earth, and it stands. They stand this day according to Your ordinances, for all things are Your servants"* (Ps. 119:89-91). God speaks out of His faithfulness, and everything leads back to and holds together in Him. He is not going to change

His mind. This gives me peace and confidence to believe all He says about Himself and me.

Desirable...Sweet—Drawing Me Close to His Heart

Finally, the voice of God carries with it sweetness. It is milk and honey to me. God has promised to bring us to the land of milk and honey. My good friend Dr. Donald Wright has said that this is the place of intimate worship of God. *"Your lips, my bride, drip honey; honey and milk are under your tongue..."* (Song 4:11). Worship is our response to the heart of God.

This psalm also tells us that His Word is "desirable." Desirable means that there is a receptivity of the Word. The tenor of God's Word does not lead to a pit of despair where we wallow in our sin and separation from God. He always brings us back to Him. If what we hear does not lead us back to God, it is not God! God doesn't condemn us, though He will frequently confront us. When God does confront us, it is because He wants to remove anything that separates us from Him. We are drawn back again to His sweetness as we are drawn to honey.

SUMMARY OF THE CHARACTER OF GOD'S VOICE AND THE EFFECT OF GOD'S VOICE

- Healing / Inviting me to God Himself.

- Clear / Allowing me to respond.

- Right / Giving me joy.

- Pure / Enlightening me about myself.

- Enduring / True, righteous, clean—giving me confidence.

- Desirable / Sweet—drawing me close, resulting in worship.

Another passage from the Word summarizes what we are saying:

*But the wisdom [whatever God speaks to us] that comes from heaven is first of all **pure**. It is also **peace loving, gentle** at all times, and **willing to yield to others**. It is **full of mercy** and good deeds. It shows **no partiality** and is always **sincere**. And those who are peacemakers will plant seeds of **peace** and reap a harvest of **goodness*** (James 3:17-18 NLT, emphasis added).

When we have *listened*, as God has *spoken* in a way that agrees with the indications we have listed, then we are free to *respond*. And anything that God is leading us into will bring glory to Him and enrapture our hearts to fall more deeply in love with Him.

When we hear the truth of God, it will reflect the character of God and bring us to the awareness of the presence of God. In His presence there is healing from all the lies and wounds that bind us. We are free to live in His presence and to enjoy rest and peace, communion, and shared purpose.

FINDING A SCRIPTURE-BASED SAFE PLACE

In this case, I will supply a sample Scripture, the passage of Mark 6 that I mentioned earlier.

*The apostles gathered around Jesus and reported to Him all they had done and taught. Then, because so many people were coming and going that they did not even have a chance to eat, He said to them, **"Come with Me by yourselves to a quiet place and get some rest"*** (Mark 6:30-31 NIV).

1. Read the whole passage a few times, then read only the lines I have highlighted in bold. What images stand out to you as you read? What do these images suggest about the heart of God? As you hold those images in your mind, make a personal connection with the Lord.

   _____

   _____

   _____

   _____

2. What is being communicated from the heart of the Lord to you? Speak that truth aloud. It may be good to write it down in your journal or even in this book. I will leave a little space to write down the words, impressions, or images that come to mind.

   _____

   _____

   _____

   _____

Dear Reader, take your time and establish a safe place to experience the presence of God. He is waiting for you there.

"TRUTH BECOMES TRUE" INSTRUCTIONS

THE TRUTH BECOMES TRUE

What was the core Truth revealed to you through today's meditation?

_____

_____

_____

_____

Watch throughout the day to see where that Truth becomes personal truth to you and journal your thoughts on this page along with other significant Truths and impressions from your travels with the Lord today.

My HEALING JOURNEY

_____

_____

_____

_____

_____

_____

_____

_____

_____

_____

PART II:

MY HEALING JOURNEY

DAY 1

THE TRUTH ABOUT FEAR— "I AM NOT ALONE"

Truth: My Father is always with me. He will never leave me.

Repeat this truth aloud. Close your eyes and rest a moment in this truth.

> [Jesus said] *"...surely I am with you always, to the very end of the age"* (Matthew 28:20 NIV).

Meditate on this Scripture, saying it to yourself softly over and over again until you can say it with your eyes closed. As you repeat the Scripture, allow yourself to see it with the eyes of your heart. What is the picture you see in your mind's eye as you repeat the Scripture?

_____

_____

_____

_____

What does the Scripture reveal about the heart of God?

_____

_____

_____

_____

What is the Lord speaking to you personally as you see the truth of this Scripture? Put yourself in the picture of this Scripture in your mind.

_____

_____

_____

_____

_____

From *Healing the Wounded Heart:* "When we run as far and hard as we can, we learn that the presence of God is already ahead of us and ready to pour out His mercy and grace."

Take time to pray, declaring to God what you have seen today.

Lord, today You said to me:

_____

_____

_____

_____

_____

_____

_____

(Please remember to enter a one-sentence synopsis in the Journal Summary section, which immediately follows the 49 daily meditations, and state what the Lord has spoken to you today.)

THE TRUTH BECOMES TRUE

What was the core Truth revealed to you through today's meditation?

_____

_____

_____

_____

Watch throughout the day to see where that Truth becomes personal truth to you and journal your thoughts on this page along with other significant Truths and impressions from your travels with the Lord today.

My HEALING JOURNEY

_____

_____

_____

_____

_____

_____

_____

_____

_____

DAY 2

THE TRUTH ABOUT FEAR—
"I AM NOT ALONE"

Truth: My Father wants to hold and comfort me when I'm afraid.

Repeat this truth aloud. Close your eyes and rest a moment in this truth.

> *As one whom his mother comforts, so I will comfort you; and you*
> *shall be comforted in Jerusalem* (Isaiah 66:13 NKJV).

Meditate on this Scripture, saying it to yourself softly over and over again until you can say it with your eyes closed. As you repeat the Scripture, allow yourself to see it with the eyes of your heart. What is the picture you see in your mind's eye as you repeat the Scripture?

_____

_____

_____

_____

What does the Scripture reveal about the heart of God?

_____

_____

_____

_____

What is the Lord speaking to you personally as you see the truth of this Scripture? Put yourself in the picture of this Scripture in your mind.

_____

_____

_____

_____

_____

From *Healing the Wounded Heart:* "We are, in effect, in the womb of God's love as He pours out His compassion upon us, bringing us to Himself and healing...."

Take time to pray, declaring to God what you have seen today.

Lord, today You said to me:

_____

_____

_____

_____

_____

_____

(Please remember to enter a one-sentence synopsis in the Journal Summary section, which immediately follows the 49 daily meditations, and state what the Lord has spoken to you today.)

THE TRUTH BECOMES TRUE

What was the core Truth revealed to you through today's meditation?

_____

_____

_____

_____

_____

Watch throughout the day to see where that Truth becomes personal truth to you and journal your thoughts on this page, along with other significant Truths and impressions from your travels with the Lord today.

My HEALING JOURNEY

_____

_____

_____

_____

_____

_____

_____

_____

_____

_____

DAY 3

THE TRUTH ABOUT FEAR—
"I AM NOT ALONE"

Truth: My Father is lovingly and faithfully watching over me.

Repeat this truth aloud. Close your eyes and rest a moment in this truth.

The Lord will watch over your coming and going both now and forevermore (Psalm 121:8 NIV).

Meditate on this Scripture, saying it to yourself softly over and over again until you can say it with your eyes closed. As you repeat the Scripture, allow yourself to see it with the eyes of your heart. What is the picture you see in your mind's eye as you repeat the Scripture?

_____

_____

_____

_____

What does the Scripture reveal about the heart of God?

_____

_____

_____

_____

What is the Lord speaking to you personally as you see the truth of this Scripture? Put yourself in the picture of this Scripture in your mind.

_____

_____

_____

_____

_____

From *Healing the Wounded Heart:* "On the day of our wounding, the Father was already leading us to the day of healing in His presence. Beloved, this is the day!"

Take time to pray, declaring to God what you have seen today.

Lord, today You said to me:

_____

_____

_____

_____

_____

_____

_____

_____

(Please remember to enter a one-sentence synopsis in the Journal Summary section, which immediately follows the 49 daily meditations, and state what the Lord has spoken to you today.)

THE TRUTH BECOMES TRUE

What was the core Truth revealed to you through today's meditation?

_____

_____

_____

_____

_____

_____

Watch throughout the day to see where that Truth becomes personal truth to you and journal your thoughts on this page along with other significant Truths and impressions from your travels with the Lord today.

My HEALING JOURNEY

_____

_____

_____

_____

_____

_____

_____

_____

_____

DAY 4

THE TRUTH ABOUT FEAR— "I AM NOT ALONE"

Truth: My Father provides all that I need in every situation.

Repeat this truth aloud. Close your eyes and rest a moment in this truth.

I can do everything through Him who gives me strength (Philippians 4:13 NIV).

Meditate on this Scripture, saying it to yourself softly over and over again until you can say it with your eyes closed. As you repeat the Scripture, allow yourself to see it with the eyes of your heart. What is the picture you see in your mind's eye as you repeat the Scripture?

_____

_____

_____

_____

What does the Scripture reveal about the heart of God?

_____

_____

_____

_____

What is the Lord speaking to you personally as you see the truth of this Scripture? Put yourself in the picture of this Scripture in your mind.

_____

_____

_____

_____

_____

From *Healing the Wounded Heart:* "We are 'secure' in the love of God and 'significant' in that God has chosen us. There can be no higher significance than to be chosen by the One who created us."

Take time to pray, declaring to God what you have seen today.

Lord, today You said to me:

_____

_____

_____

_____

_____

_____

_____

_____

(Please remember to enter a one-sentence synopsis in the Journal Summary section, which immediately follows the 49 daily meditations, and state what the Lord has spoken to you today.)

THE TRUTH BECOMES TRUE

What was the core Truth revealed to you through today's meditation?

_____

_____

_____

_____

_____

_____

Watch throughout the day to see where that Truth becomes personal truth to you and journal your thoughts on this page along with other significant Truths and impressions from your travels with the Lord today.

My HEALING JOURNEY

_____

_____

_____

_____

_____

_____

_____

_____

_____

_____

_____

DAY 5

THE TRUTH ABOUT FEAR— "I AM NOT ALONE"

Truth: The Father is always present to help me.

Repeat this truth aloud. Close your eyes and rest a moment in this truth.

> *So do not fear, for I am with you; do not be dismayed, for I am your God. I will strengthen you and help you; I will uphold you with My righteous right hand* (Isaiah 41:10 NIV).

Meditate on this Scripture, saying it to yourself softly over and over again until you can say it with your eyes closed. As you repeat the Scripture, allow yourself to see it with the eyes of your heart. What is the picture you see in your mind's eye as you repeat the Scripture?

_____

_____

_____

What does the Scripture reveal about the heart of God?

_____

_____

_____

_____

What is the Lord speaking to you personally as you see the truth of this Scripture? Put yourself in the picture of this Scripture in your mind.

_____

_____

_____

_____

_____

From *Healing the Wounded Heart:* "We are totally enclosed and protected between His hands. God holds the past, future, and present firmly and tenderly in the grip of His hand..."

Take time to pray, declaring to God what you have seen today.

Lord, today You said to me:

_____

_____

_____

_____

_____

_____

_____

(Please remember to enter a one-sentence synopsis in the Journal Summary section, which immediately follows the 49 daily meditations, and state what the Lord has spoken to you today.)

THE TRUTH BECOMES TRUE

What was the core Truth revealed to you through today's meditation?

_____

_____

_____

_____

_____

_____

Watch throughout the day to see where that Truth becomes personal truth to you and journal your thoughts on this page along with other significant Truths and impressions from your travels with the Lord today.

My HEALING JOURNEY

_____

_____

_____

_____

_____

_____

_____

_____

_____

_____

DAY 6

THE TRUTH ABOUT FEAR— "I AM NOT ALONE"

Truth: I can rest in the strong and capable arms of my Father.

Repeat this truth aloud. Close your eyes and rest a moment in this truth.

The eternal God is your refuge, and underneath are the everlasting arms (Deuteronomy 33:27 NIV).

Meditate on this Scripture, saying it to yourself softly over and over again until you can say it with your eyes closed. As you repeat the Scripture, allow yourself to see it with the eyes of your heart. What is the picture you see in your mind's eye as you repeat the Scripture?

_____

_____

_____

_____

What does the Scripture reveal about the heart of God?

_____

_____

_____

_____

What is the Lord speaking to you personally as you see the truth of this Scripture? Put yourself in the picture of this Scripture in your mind.

_____

_____

_____

_____

_____

From *Healing the Wounded Heart:* "God is a compassionate and gracious God who speaks to the little children in us, inviting us to healing in His embrace."

Take time to pray, declaring to God what you have seen today.

Lord, today You said to me:

_____

_____

_____

_____

_____

_____

_____

_____

(Please remember to enter a one-sentence synopsis in the Journal Summary section, which immediately follows the 49 daily meditations, and state what the Lord has spoken to you today.)

THE TRUTH BECOMES TRUE

What was the core Truth revealed to you through today's meditation?

_____

_____

_____

_____

_____

_____

Watch throughout the day to see where that Truth becomes personal truth to you and journal your thoughts on this page along with other significant Truths and impressions from your travels with the Lord today.

My HEALING JOURNEY

_____

_____

_____

_____

_____

_____

_____

_____

_____

_____

DAY 7

THE TRUTH ABOUT FEAR— "I AM NOT ALONE"

Truth: My Father is always there for me. He wants me to trust Him.

Repeat this truth aloud. Close your eyes and rest a moment in this truth.

> *Trust in the Lord with all your heart and lean not on your own understanding; in all your ways acknowledge Him, and He will make your paths straight* (Proverbs 3:5-6 NIV).

Meditate on this Scripture, saying it to yourself softly over and over again until you can say it with your eyes closed. As you repeat the Scripture, allow yourself to see it with the eyes of your heart. What is the picture you see in your mind's eye as you repeat the Scripture?

_____

_____

_____

What does the Scripture reveal about the heart of God?

_____

_____

_____

_____

What is the Lord speaking to you personally as you see the truth of this Scripture? Put yourself in the picture of this Scripture in your mind.

_____

_____

_____

_____

_____

From *Healing the Wounded Heart:* "...the presence of God is the source of all healing. It is really what we all long for."

Take time to pray, declaring to God what you have seen today.

Lord, today You said to me:

_____

_____

_____

_____

_____

_____

_____

_____

_____

(Please remember to enter a one-sentence synopsis in the Journal Summary section, which immediately follows the 49 daily meditations, and state what the Lord has spoken to you today.)

THE TRUTH BECOMES TRUE

What was the core Truth revealed to you through today's meditation?

_____

_____

_____

_____

_____

_____

Watch throughout the day to see where that Truth becomes personal truth to you and journal your thoughts on this page along with other significant Truths and impressions from your travels with the Lord today.

My HEALING JOURNEY

_____

_____

_____

_____

_____

_____

_____

_____

_____

DAY 8

THE TRUTH ABOUT REJECTION—
"I AM ACCEPTED BY MY FATHER"

Truth: I am chosen, treasured, and loved.

Repeat this truth aloud. Close your eyes and rest a moment in this truth.

> *The Lord has today declared you to be His people, a treasured possession, as He promised you, and that you should keep all His commandments* (Deuteronomy 26:18).

Meditate on this Scripture, saying it to yourself softly over and over again until you can say it with your eyes closed. As you repeat the Scripture, allow yourself to see it with the eyes of your heart. What is the picture you see in your mind's eye as you repeat the Scripture?

_____

_____

_____

What does the Scripture reveal about the heart of God?

_____

_____

_____

_____

What is the Lord speaking to you personally as you see the truth of this Scripture? Put yourself in the picture of this Scripture in your mind.

_____

_____

_____

_____

_____

From *Healing the Wounded Heart:* "God has chosen us and loved us simply because He desires to do so."

Take time to pray, declaring to God what you have seen today.

Lord, today You said to me:

_____

_____

_____

_____

_____

_____

_____

_____

_____

(Please remember to enter a one-sentence synopsis in the Journal Summary section, which immediately follows the 49 daily meditations, and state what the Lord has spoken to you today.)

THE TRUTH BECOMES TRUE

What was the core Truth revealed to you through today's meditation?

_____

_____

_____

_____

_____

_____

Watch throughout the day to see where that Truth becomes personal truth to you and journal your thoughts on this page along with other significant Truths and impressions from your travels with the Lord today.

My HEALING JOURNEY

_____

_____

_____

_____

_____

_____

_____

_____

_____

_____

DAY 9

THE TRUTH ABOUT REJECTION— "I AM ACCEPTED BY MY FATHER"

Truth: I am a child of the Father.

Repeat this truth aloud. Close your eyes and rest a moment in this truth.

> *The Spirit Himself testifies with our spirit that we are children of God, and if children, heirs also, heirs of God and fellow heirs with Christ...* (Romans 8:16-17).

Meditate on this Scripture, saying it to yourself softly over and over again until you can say it with your eyes closed. As you repeat the Scripture, allow yourself to see it with the eyes of your heart. What is the picture you see in your mind's eye as you repeat the Scripture?

_____

_____

_____

What does the Scripture reveal about the heart of God?

_____

_____

_____

_____

What is the Lord speaking to you personally as you see the truth of this Scripture? Put yourself in the picture of this Scripture in your mind.

_____

_____

_____

_____

_____

From *Healing the Wounded Heart:* "He [Jesus] is inviting that little wounded one in you into His presence to wipe away your tears and tell you the truth about yourself."

Take time to pray, declaring to God what you have seen today.

Lord, today You said to me:

_____

_____

_____

_____

_____

_____

_____

_____

(Please remember to enter a one-sentence synopsis in the Journal Summary section, which immediately follows the 49 daily meditations, and state what the Lord has spoken to you today.)

THE TRUTH BECOMES TRUE

What was the core Truth revealed to you through today's meditation?

_____

_____

_____

_____

_____

_____

Watch throughout the day to see where that Truth becomes personal truth to you and journal your thoughts on this page along with other significant Truths and impressions from your travels with the Lord today.

My HEALING JOURNEY

_____

_____

_____

_____

_____

_____

_____

_____

_____

_____

_____

DAY 10

THE TRUTH ABOUT REJECTION— "I AM ACCEPTED BY MY FATHER"

Truth: I belong to the Father.

Repeat this truth aloud. Close your eyes and rest a moment in this truth.

But now, this is what the Lord says—He who created you, O Jacob, He who formed you, O Israel: "Fear not, for I have redeemed you; I have summoned you by name; you are Mine" (Isaiah 43:1 NIV).

Meditate on this Scripture, saying it to yourself softly over and over again until you can say it with your eyes closed. As you repeat the Scripture, allow yourself to see it with the eyes of your heart. What is the picture you see in your mind's eye as you repeat the Scripture?

_____

_____

What does the Scripture reveal about the heart of God?

_____

_____

_____

_____

What is the Lord speaking to you personally as you see the truth of this Scripture? Put yourself in the picture of this Scripture in your mind.

_____

_____

_____

_____

_____

From *Healing the Wounded Heart:* "It is possible that others may have turned their backs on us, but Jesus stands with arms open wide to receive us."

Take time to pray, declaring to God what you have seen today.

Lord, today You said to me:

_____

_____

_____

_____

_____

_____

_____

_____

_____

(Please remember to enter a one-sentence synopsis in the Journal Summary section, which immediately follows the 49 daily meditations, and state what the Lord has spoken to you today.)

THE TRUTH BECOMES TRUE

What was the core Truth revealed to you through today's meditation?

_____

_____

_____

_____

_____

Watch throughout the day to see where that Truth becomes personal truth to you and journal your thoughts on this page along with other significant Truths and impressions from your travels with the Lord today.

My HEALING JOURNEY

_____

_____

_____

_____

_____

_____

_____

_____

_____

DAY 11

THE TRUTH ABOUT REJECTION— "I AM ACCEPTED BY MY FATHER"

Truth: I am Christ's friend.

Repeat this truth aloud. Close your eyes and rest a moment in this truth.

> *I no longer call you servants, because a servant does not know his master's business. Instead, I have called you friends, for everything that I learned from My Father I have made known to you* (John 15:15 NIV).

Meditate on this Scripture, saying it to yourself softly over and over again until you can say it with your eyes closed. As you repeat the Scripture, allow yourself to see it with the eyes of your heart. What is the picture you see in your mind's eye as you repeat the Scripture?

_____

_____

What does the Scripture reveal about the heart of God?

_____

_____

_____

_____

What is the Lord speaking to you personally as you see the truth of this Scripture? Put yourself in the picture of this Scripture in your mind.

_____

_____

_____

_____

_____

From *Healing the Wounded Heart:* "It is our relationship with Christ that distinguishes us from all others. It is our position in Christ that determines our worth and purpose."

Take time to pray, declaring to God what you have seen today.

Lord, today You said to me:

_____

_____

_____

_____

_____

_____

_____

(Please remember to enter a one-sentence synopsis in the Journal Summary section, which immediately follows the 49 daily meditations, and state what the Lord has spoken to you today.)

THE TRUTH BECOMES TRUE

What was the core Truth revealed to you through today's meditation?

_____

_____

_____

_____

_____

_____

Watch throughout the day to see where that Truth becomes personal truth to you and journal your thoughts on this page along with other significant Truths and impressions from your travels with the Lord today.

My HEALING JOURNEY

_____

_____

_____

_____

_____

_____

_____

_____

_____

_____

DAY 12

THE TRUTH ABOUT REJECTION— "I AM ACCEPTED BY MY FATHER"

Truth: The Father is always for me, never against me.

Repeat this truth aloud. Close your eyes and rest a moment in this truth.

What, then, shall we say in response to this? If God is for us, who can be against us? (Romans 8:31 NIV)

Meditate on this Scripture, saying it to yourself softly over and over again until you can say it with your eyes closed. As you repeat the Scripture, allow yourself to see it with the eyes of your heart. What is the picture you see in your mind's eye as you repeat the Scripture?

_____

_____

_____

_____

What does the Scripture reveal about the heart of God?

_____

_____

_____

_____

What is the Lord speaking to you personally as you see the truth of this Scripture? Put yourself in the picture of this Scripture in your mind.

_____

_____

_____

_____

_____

From *Healing the Wounded Heart:* "There is no night too dark, no shore too distant, for the presence and compassion of God."

Take time to pray, declaring to God what you have seen today.

Lord, today You said to me:

_____

_____

_____

_____

_____

_____

_____

_____

_____

_____

(Please remember to enter a one-sentence synopsis in the Journal Summary section, which immediately follows the 49 daily meditations, and state what the Lord has spoken to you today.)

THE TRUTH BECOMES TRUE

What was the core Truth revealed to you through today's meditation?

_____

_____

_____

_____

_____

_____

Watch throughout the day to see where that Truth becomes personal truth to you and journal your thoughts on this page along with other significant Truths and impressions from your travels with the Lord today.

My HEALING JOURNEY

_____

_____

_____

_____

_____

_____

_____

_____

_____

_____

DAY 13

THE TRUTH ABOUT REJECTION— "I AM ACCEPTED BY MY FATHER"

Truth: My Father will never forget me. I have always been loved by Him. Repeat this truth aloud. Close your eyes and rest a moment in this truth.

> *Can a mother forget the baby at her breast and have no compassion on the child she has borne? Though she may forget, I will not forget you! See, I have engraved you on the palms of My hands...* (Isaiah 49:15-16 NIV).

Meditate on this Scripture, saying it to yourself softly over and over again until you can say it with your eyes closed. As you repeat the Scripture, allow yourself to see it with the eyes of your heart. What is the picture you see in your mind's eye as you repeat the Scripture?

_____

_____

What does the Scripture reveal about the heart of God?

_____

_____

_____

_____

What is the Lord speaking to you personally as you see the truth of this Scripture? Put yourself in the picture of this Scripture in your mind.

_____

_____

_____

_____

_____

From *Healing the Wounded Heart:* "To those of you who have lived on the edge of the camp, in the outer cold away from the fire, God has brought the fire to you."

Take time to pray, declaring to God what you have seen today.

Lord, today You said to me:

_____

_____

_____

_____

_____

_____

_____

(Please remember to enter a one-sentence synopsis in the Journal Summary section, which immediately follows the 49 daily meditations, and state what the Lord has spoken to you today.)

THE TRUTH BECOMES TRUE

What was the core Truth revealed to you through today's meditation?

_____

_____

_____

_____

_____

Watch throughout the day to see where that Truth becomes personal truth to you and journal your thoughts on this page along with other significant Truths and impressions from your travels with the Lord today.

My HEALING JOURNEY

_____

_____

_____

_____

_____

_____

_____

_____

_____

_____

DAY 14

THE TRUTH ABOUT REJECTION—
"I AM ACCEPTED BY MY FATHER"

Truth: Troubles do not separate me from Father's love.

Repeat this truth aloud. Close your eyes and rest a moment in this truth.

> *Who shall separate us from the love of Christ? Shall trouble or hardship or persecution or famine or nakedness or danger or sword?...nor anything else in all creation, will be able to separate us from the love of God that is in Christ Jesus our Lord* (Romans 8:35,39 NIV).

Meditate on this Scripture, saying it to yourself softly over and over again until you can say it with your eyes closed. As you repeat the Scripture, allow yourself to see it with the eyes of your heart. What is the picture you see in your mind's eye as you repeat the Scripture?

_____

_____

What does the Scripture reveal about the heart of God?

_____

_____

_____

What is the Lord speaking to you personally as you see the truth of this Scripture? Put yourself in the picture of this Scripture in your mind.

_____

_____

_____

_____

_____

From *Healing the Wounded Heart:* "We were created to live in His presence, literally His face, with nothing between our face and His."

Take time to pray, declaring to God what you have seen today.

Lord, today You said to me:

_____

_____

_____

_____

_____

_____

_____

_____

_____

(Please remember to enter a one-sentence synopsis in the Journal Summary section, which immediately follows the 49 daily meditations, and state what the Lord has spoken to you today.)

THE TRUTH BECOMES TRUE

What was the core Truth revealed to you through today's meditation?

_____

_____

_____

_____

_____

_____

Watch throughout the day to see where that Truth becomes personal truth to you and journal your thoughts on this page along with other significant Truths and impressions from your travels with the Lord today.

My HEALING JOURNEY

_____

_____

_____

_____

_____

_____

_____

_____

_____

_____

_____

DAY 15

THE TRUTH ABOUT WORTHLESSNESS— "THE FATHER APPROVES OF ME"

Truth: I am a unique creation of the Father. I am handmade. In all the world there's no one else like me.

Repeat this truth aloud. Close your eyes and rest a moment in this truth.

> *I praise You because I am fearfully and wonderfully made; Your works are wonderful, I know that full well* (Psalm 139:14 NIV).

Meditate on this Scripture, saying it to yourself softly over and over again until you can say it with your eyes closed. As you repeat the Scripture, allow yourself to see it with the eyes of your heart. What is the picture you see in your mind's eye as you repeat the Scripture?

_____

_____

_____

What does the Scripture reveal about the heart of God?

_____

_____

_____

_____

What is the Lord speaking to you personally as you see the truth of this Scripture? Put yourself in the picture of this Scripture in your mind.

_____

_____

_____

_____

_____

From *Healing the Wounded Heart:* "God does not compare us with any other person. We are handmade originals...we are Stradivarius violins, priceless and incomparable."

Take time to pray, declaring to God what you have seen today.

Lord, today You said to me:

_____

_____

_____

_____

_____

_____

_____

_____

(Please remember to enter a one-sentence synopsis in the Journal Summary section, which immediately follows the 49 daily meditations, and state what the Lord has spoken to you today.)

THE TRUTH BECOMES TRUE

What was the core Truth revealed to you through today's meditation?

_____

_____

_____

_____

_____

_____

Watch throughout the day to see where that Truth becomes personal truth to you and journal your thoughts on this page along with other significant Truths and impressions from your travels with the Lord today.

My HEALING JOURNEY

_____

_____

_____

_____

_____

_____

_____

_____

_____

DAY 16

THE TRUTH ABOUT WORTHLESSNESS— "THE FATHER APPROVES OF ME"

Truth: I am loved and treasured by the Creator of the universe.

Repeat this truth aloud. Close your eyes and rest a moment in this truth.

> *The Lord appeared to us in the past, saying: "I have loved you with an everlasting love; I have drawn you with loving-kindness"* (Jeremiah 31:3 NIV).

Meditate on this Scripture, saying it to yourself softly over and over again until you can say it with your eyes closed. As you repeat the Scripture, allow yourself to see it with the eyes of your heart. What is the picture you see in your mind's eye as you repeat the Scripture?

_____

_____

_____

What does the Scripture reveal about the heart of God?

_____

_____

_____

_____

What is the Lord speaking to you personally as you see the truth of this Scripture? Put yourself in the picture of this Scripture in your mind.

_____

_____

_____

_____

_____

From *Healing the Wounded Heart:* "Each of us is a special creation of God. What is important to God seldom appears important to man."

Take time to pray, declaring to God what you have seen today.

Lord, today You said to me:

_____

_____

_____

_____

_____

_____

_____

_____

_____

_____

_____

(Please remember to enter a one-sentence synopsis in the Journal Summary section, which immediately follows the 49 daily meditations, and state what the Lord has spoken to you today.)

THE TRUTH BECOMES TRUE

What was the core Truth revealed to you through today's meditation?

_____

_____

_____

_____

_____

_____

Watch throughout the day to see where that Truth becomes personal truth to you and journal your thoughts on this page along with other significant Truths and impressions from your travels with the Lord today.

My HEALING JOURNEY

_____

_____

_____

_____

_____

_____

_____

_____

_____

_____

_____

DAY 17

THE TRUTH ABOUT WORTHLESSNESS— "THE FATHER APPROVES OF ME"

Truth: I am important and valuable.

Repeat this truth aloud. Close your eyes and rest a moment in this truth.

> *In a desert land He found him, in a barren and howling waste.*
> *He shielded him and cared for him; He guarded him as the*
> *apple of His eye* (Deuteronomy 32:10 NIV).

Meditate on this Scripture, saying it to yourself softly over and over again until you can say it with your eyes closed. As you repeat the Scripture, allow yourself to see it with the eyes of your heart. What is the picture you see in your mind's eye as you repeat the Scripture?

_____

_____

_____

What does the Scripture reveal about the heart of God?

_____

_____

_____

_____

What is the Lord speaking to you personally as you see the truth of this Scripture? Put yourself in the picture of this Scripture in your mind.

_____

_____

_____

_____

_____

From *Healing the Wounded Heart:* "...we are incomparable to any other person ever made. We are as original and unique as our fingerprints."

Take time to pray, declaring to God what you have seen today.

Lord, today You said to me:

_____

_____

_____

_____

_____

_____

_____

_____

_____

_____

(Please remember to enter a one-sentence synopsis in the Journal Summary section, which immediately follows the 49 daily meditations, and state what the Lord has spoken to you today.)

THE TRUTH BECOMES TRUE

What was the core Truth revealed to you through today's meditation?

_____

_____

_____

_____

_____

_____

Watch throughout the day to see where that Truth becomes personal truth to you and journal your thoughts on this page along with other significant Truths and impressions from your travels with the Lord today.

My HEALING JOURNEY

_____

_____

_____

_____

_____

_____

_____

_____

_____

_____

DAY 18

THE TRUTH ABOUT WORTHLESSNESS— "THE FATHER APPROVES OF ME"

Truth: I am precious and honored in the eyes of my Father.

Repeat this truth aloud. Close your eyes and rest a moment in this truth.

Since you are precious and honored in My sight, and because I love you... (Isaiah 43:4 NIV).

Meditate on this Scripture, saying it to yourself softly over and over again until you can say it with your eyes closed. As you repeat the Scripture, allow yourself to see it with the eyes of your heart. What is the picture you see in your mind's eye as you repeat the Scripture?

_____

_____

_____

_____

What does the Scripture reveal about the heart of God?

_____

_____

_____

_____

What is the Lord speaking to you personally as you see the truth of this Scripture? Put yourself in the picture of this Scripture in your mind.

_____

_____

_____

_____

_____

From *Healing the Wounded Heart:* "As God's irreplaceable and handmade creations, we cannot be compared to any other. We belong to Him."

Take time to pray, declaring to God what you have seen today.

Lord, today You said to me:

_____

_____

_____

_____

_____

_____

_____

_____

_____

(Please remember to enter a one-sentence synopsis in the Journal Summary section, which immediately follows the 49 daily meditations, and state what the Lord has spoken to you today.)

THE TRUTH BECOMES TRUE

What was the core Truth revealed to you through today's meditation?

_____

_____

_____

_____

_____

_____

Watch throughout the day to see where that Truth becomes personal truth to you and journal your thoughts on this page along with other significant Truths and impressions from your travels with the Lord today.

My HEALING JOURNEY

_____

_____

_____

_____

_____

_____

_____

_____

_____

DAY 19

THE TRUTH ABOUT WORTHLESSNESS— "THE FATHER APPROVES OF ME"

Truth: The Father loves me completely, thoroughly, and perfectly. There's nothing I can do to add or detract from that love.

Repeat this truth aloud. Close your eyes and rest a moment in this truth.

> *"Though the mountains be shaken and the hills be removed, yet My unfailing love for you will not be shaken nor My covenant of peace be removed," says the Lord, who has compassion on you* (Isaiah 54:10 NIV).

Meditate on this Scripture, saying it to yourself softly over and over again until you can say it with your eyes closed. As you repeat the Scripture, allow yourself to see it with the eyes of your heart. What is the picture you see in your mind's eye as you repeat the Scripture?

_____

_____

What does the Scripture reveal about the heart of God?

_____

_____

_____

What is the Lord speaking to you personally as you see the truth of this Scripture? Put yourself in the picture of this Scripture in your mind.

_____

_____

_____

_____

_____

From *Healing the Wounded Heart:* "God does not see things in the carnal comparative way that we do, any more than we see our own children in that way."

Take time to pray, declaring to God what you have seen today.

Lord, today You said to me:

_____

_____

_____

_____

_____

_____

_____

_____

(Please remember to enter a one-sentence synopsis in the Journal Summary section, which immediately follows the 49 daily meditations, and state what the Lord has spoken to you today.)

THE TRUTH BECOMES TRUE

What was the core Truth revealed to you through today's meditation?

_____

_____

_____

_____

_____

Watch throughout the day to see where that Truth becomes personal truth to you and journal your thoughts on this page along with other significant Truths and impressions from your travels with the Lord today.

My HEALING JOURNEY

_____

_____

_____

_____

_____

_____

_____

_____

_____

DAY 20

THE TRUTH ABOUT WORTHLESSNESS— "THE FATHER APPROVES OF ME"

Truth: My life has a purpose.

Repeat this truth aloud. Close your eyes and rest a moment in this truth.

> *And He has committed to us the message of reconciliation. We are therefore Christ's ambassadors...* (2 Corinthians 5:19-20 NIV).

Meditate on this Scripture, saying it to yourself softly over and over again until you can say it with your eyes closed. As you repeat the Scripture, allow yourself to see it with the eyes of your heart. What is the picture you see in your mind's eye as you repeat the Scripture?

_____

_____

_____

What does the Scripture reveal about the heart of God?

_____

_____

_____

_____

What is the Lord speaking to you personally as you see the truth of this Scripture? Put yourself in the picture of this Scripture in your mind.

_____

_____

_____

_____

_____

From *Healing the Wounded Heart:* "Those in Christ exist for the purpose of fellowship with God, giving Him glory through their lives."

Take time to pray, declaring to God what you have seen today.

Lord, today You said to me:

_____

_____

_____

_____

_____

_____

_____

_____

(Please remember to enter a one-sentence synopsis in the Journal Summary section, which immediately follows the 49 daily meditations, and state what the Lord has spoken to you today.)

THE TRUTH BECOMES TRUE

What was the core Truth revealed to you through today's meditation?

_____

_____

_____

_____

_____

_____

Watch throughout the day to see where that Truth becomes personal truth to you and journal your thoughts on this page along with other significant Truths and impressions from your travels with the Lord today.

My HEALING JOURNEY

_____

_____

_____

_____

_____

_____

_____

_____

_____

_____

DAY 21

THE TRUTH ABOUT WORTHLESSNESS— "THE FATHER APPROVES OF ME"

Truth: The Father celebrates my life! He delights in me.

Repeat this truth aloud. Close your eyes and rest a moment in this truth.

> *The Lord your God is with you, He is mighty to save. He will take great delight in you, He will quiet you with His love, He will rejoice over you with singing* (Zephaniah 3:17 NIV).

Meditate on this Scripture, saying it to yourself softly over and over again until you can say it with your eyes closed. As you repeat the Scripture, allow yourself to see it with the eyes of your heart. What is the picture you see in your mind's eye as you repeat the Scripture?

_____

_____

_____

What does the Scripture reveal about the heart of God?

_____

_____

_____

_____

What is the Lord speaking to you personally as you see the truth of this Scripture? Put yourself in the picture of this Scripture in your mind.

_____

_____

_____

_____

_____

From *Healing the Wounded Heart:* "Beloved, the Lord has passion for our little faces."

Take time to pray, declaring to God what you have seen today.

Lord, today You said to me:

_____

_____

_____

_____

_____

_____

_____

_____

(Please remember to enter a one-sentence synopsis in the Journal Summary section, which immediately follows the 49 daily meditations, and state what the Lord has spoken to you today.)

THE TRUTH BECOMES TRUE

What was the core Truth revealed to you through today's meditation?

_____

_____

_____

_____

_____

Watch throughout the day to see where that Truth becomes personal truth to you and journal your thoughts on this page along with other significant Truths and impressions from your travels with the Lord today.

My HEALING JOURNEY

_____

_____

_____

_____

_____

_____

_____

_____

_____

DAY 22

THE TRUTH ABOUT SHAME—
"I AM COVERED WITH CHRIST"

Truth: I am enough. I am absolutely complete in Christ.

Repeat this truth aloud. Close your eyes and rest a moment in this truth.

> *But He said to me, "My grace is sufficient for you, for My power is made perfect in weakness." Therefore I will boast all the more gladly about my weaknesses, so that Christ's power may rest on me* (2 Corinthians 12:9 NIV).

Meditate on this Scripture, saying it to yourself softly over and over again until you can say it with your eyes closed. As you repeat the Scripture, allow yourself to see it with the eyes of your heart. What is the picture you see in your mind's eye as you repeat the Scripture?

_____

_____

_____

What does the Scripture reveal about the heart of God?

_____

_____

_____

What is the Lord speaking to you personally as you see the truth of this Scripture? Put yourself in the picture of this Scripture in your mind.

_____

_____

_____

_____

_____

From *Healing the Wounded Heart:* "God sees us as we see our children—as His own precious possessions."

Take time to pray, declaring to God what you have seen today.

Lord, today You said to me:

_____

_____

_____

_____

_____

_____

_____

(Please remember to enter a one-sentence synopsis in the Journal Summary section, which immediately follows the 49 daily meditations, and state what the Lord has spoken to you today.)

THE TRUTH BECOMES TRUE

What was the core Truth revealed to you through today's meditation?

_____

_____

_____

_____

_____

Watch throughout the day to see where that Truth becomes personal truth to you and journal your thoughts on this page along with other significant Truths and impressions from your travels with the Lord today.

My HEALING JOURNEY

_____

_____

_____

_____

_____

_____

_____

_____

_____

_____

DAY 23

THE TRUTH ABOUT SHAME— "I AM COVERED WITH CHRIST"

Truth: I am totally covered.

Repeat this truth aloud. Close your eyes and rest a moment in this truth.

> *I will rejoice greatly in the Lord, my soul will exult in my God; for He has clothed me with garments of salvation, He has wrapped me with a robe of righteousness* (Isaiah 61:10).

Meditate on this Scripture, saying it to yourself softly over and over again until you can say it with your eyes closed. As you repeat the Scripture, allow yourself to see it with the eyes of your heart. What is the picture you see in your mind's eye as you repeat the Scripture?

_____

_____

_____

What does the Scripture reveal about the heart of God?

_____

_____

_____

_____

What is the Lord speaking to you personally as you see the truth of this Scripture? Put yourself in the picture of this Scripture in your mind.

_____

_____

_____

_____

From *Healing the Wounded Heart:* "He took our nakedness upon Himself so that we could be clothed with His own righteousness."

Take time to pray, declaring to God what you have seen today.

Lord, today You said to me:

_____

_____

_____

_____

_____

_____

_____

_____

(Please remember to enter a one-sentence synopsis in the Journal Summary section, which immediately follows the 49 daily meditations, and state what the Lord has spoken to you today.)

THE TRUTH BECOMES TRUE

What was the core Truth revealed to you through today's meditation?

_____

_____

_____

_____

_____

_____

Watch throughout the day to see where that Truth becomes personal truth to you and journal your thoughts on this page along with other significant Truths and impressions from your travels with the Lord today.

My HEALING JOURNEY

_____

_____

_____

_____

_____

_____

_____

_____

_____

_____

DAY 24

THE TRUTH ABOUT SHAME— "I AM COVERED WITH CHRIST"

Truth: My Father has forgiven and forgotten my sin.

Repeat this truth aloud. Close your eyes and rest a moment in this truth.

> *I, even I, am He who blots out your transgressions, for My own sake, and remembers your sins no more* (Isaiah 43:25 NIV).

Meditate on this Scripture, saying it to yourself softly over and over again until you can say it with your eyes closed. As you repeat the Scripture, allow yourself to see it with the eyes of your heart. What is the picture you see in your mind's eye as you repeat the Scripture?

_____

_____

_____

_____

What does the Scripture reveal about the heart of God?

_____

_____

_____

_____

What is the Lord speaking to you personally as you see the truth of this Scripture? Put yourself in the picture of this Scripture in your mind.

_____

_____

_____

_____

_____

From *Healing the Wounded Heart:* "...stop crying over spilled milk and let the Lord remove the shame that prevents you from fellowshipping with Him."

Take time to pray, declaring to God what you have seen today.

Lord, today You said to me:

_____

_____

_____

_____

_____

_____

_____

_____

(Please remember to enter a one-sentence synopsis in the Journal Summary section, which immediately follows the 49 daily meditations, and state what the Lord has spoken to you today.)

THE TRUTH BECOMES TRUE

What was the core Truth revealed to you through today's meditation?

_____

_____

_____

_____

_____

Watch throughout the day to see where that Truth becomes personal truth to you and journal your thoughts on this page along with other significant Truths and impressions from your travels with the Lord today.

My HEALING JOURNEY

_____

_____

_____

_____

_____

_____

_____

_____

_____

DAY 25

THE TRUTH ABOUT SHAME—
"I AM COVERED WITH CHRIST"

Truth: Nothing can separate me from God's love.

Repeat this truth aloud. Close your eyes and rest a moment in this truth.

> *Where can I go from Your Spirit? Or where can I flee from Your presence?* (Psalm 139:7)

Meditate on this Scripture, saying it to yourself softly over and over again until you can say it with your eyes closed. As you repeat the Scripture, allow yourself to see it with the eyes of your heart. What is the picture you see in your mind's eye as you repeat the Scripture?

_____

_____

_____

_____

What does the Scripture reveal about the heart of God?

_____

_____

_____

_____

What is the Lord speaking to you personally as you see the truth of this Scripture? Put yourself in the picture of this Scripture in your mind.

_____

_____

_____

_____

_____

From *Healing the Wounded Heart:* "God is not satisfied to leave us in the bushes. He calls to us and invites us to repentance and restoration in His presence."

Take time to pray, declaring to God what you have seen today.

Lord, today You said to me:

_____

_____

_____

_____

_____

_____

_____

(Please remember to enter a one-sentence synopsis in the Journal Summary section, which immediately follows the 49 daily meditations, and state what the Lord has spoken to you today.)

THE TRUTH BECOMES TRUE

What was the core Truth revealed to you through today's meditation?

_____

_____

_____

_____

_____

_____

Watch throughout the day to see where that Truth becomes personal truth to you and journal your thoughts on this page along with other significant Truths and impressions from your travels with the Lord today.

My HEALING JOURNEY

_____

_____

_____

_____

_____

_____

_____

_____

_____

_____

_____

DAY 26

THE TRUTH ABOUT SHAME— "I AM COVERED WITH CHRIST"

Truth: I am free from condemnation.

Repeat this truth aloud. Close your eyes and rest a moment in this truth.

> *Therefore, there is now no condemnation for those who are in Christ Jesus, because through Christ Jesus the law of the Spirit of life set me free from the law of sin and death* (Romans 8:1-2 NIV).

Meditate on this Scripture, saying it to yourself softly over and over again until you can say it with your eyes closed. As you repeat the Scripture, allow yourself to see it with the eyes of your heart. What is the picture you see in your mind's eye as you repeat the Scripture?

_____

_____

What does the Scripture reveal about the heart of God?

_____

_____

_____

_____

What is the Lord speaking to you personally as you see the truth of this Scripture? Put yourself in the picture of this Scripture in your mind.

_____

_____

_____

_____

_____

From *Healing the Wounded Heart:* "God's response (to our sin) is to call us back into intimate fellowship."

Take time to pray, declaring to God what you have seen today.

Lord, today You said to me:

_____

_____

_____

_____

_____

_____

_____

_____

_____

(Please remember to enter a one-sentence synopsis in the Journal Summary section, which immediately follows the 49 daily meditations, and state what the Lord has spoken to you today.)

THE TRUTH BECOMES TRUE

What was the core Truth revealed to you through today's meditation?

_____

_____

_____

_____

_____

_____

Watch throughout the day to see where that Truth becomes personal truth to you and journal your thoughts on this page along with other significant Truths and impressions from your travels with the Lord today.

My HEALING JOURNEY

_____

_____

_____

_____

_____

_____

_____

_____

_____

_____

_____

DAY 27

THE TRUTH ABOUT SHAME— "I AM COVERED WITH CHRIST"

Truth: Jesus is not ashamed of me.

Repeat this truth aloud. Close your eyes and rest a moment in this truth.

Both the one who makes men holy and those who are made holy are of the same family. So Jesus is not ashamed to call them brothers (Hebrews 2:11 NIV).

Meditate on this Scripture, saying it to yourself softly over and over again until you can say it with your eyes closed. As you repeat the Scripture, allow yourself to see it with the eyes of your heart. What is the picture you see in your mind's eye as you repeat the Scripture?

_____

_____

_____

What does the Scripture reveal about the heart of God?

_____

_____

_____

What is the Lord speaking to you personally as you see the truth of this Scripture? Put yourself in the picture of this Scripture in your mind.

_____

_____

_____

_____

_____

From *Healing the Wounded Heart:* "The message is clear: No one should be kept from the table of God's grace."

Take time to pray, declaring to God what you have seen today.

Lord, today You said to me:

_____

_____

_____

_____

_____

_____

_____

_____

_____

(Please remember to enter a one-sentence synopsis in the Journal Summary section, which immediately follows the 49 daily meditations, and state what the Lord has spoken to you today.)

THE TRUTH BECOMES TRUE

What was the core Truth revealed to you through today's meditation?

_____

_____

_____

_____

_____

Watch throughout the day to see where that Truth becomes personal truth to you and journal your thoughts on this page along with other significant Truths and impressions from your travels with the Lord today.

My HEALING JOURNEY

_____

_____

_____

_____

_____

_____

_____

_____

_____

DAY 28

THE TRUTH ABOUT SHAME— "I AM COVERED WITH CHRIST"

Truth: I have been made holy through Christ.

Repeat this truth aloud. Close your eyes and rest a moment in this truth.

> *But now He has reconciled you by Christ's physical body through death to present you holy in His sight, without blemish and free from accusation* (Colossians 1:22 NIV).

Meditate on this Scripture, saying it to yourself softly over and over again until you can say it with your eyes closed. As you repeat the Scripture, allow yourself to see it with the eyes of your heart. What is the picture you see in your mind's eye as you repeat the Scripture?

_____

_____

_____

What does the Scripture reveal about the heart of God?

_____

_____

_____

_____

What is the Lord speaking to you personally as you see the truth of this Scripture? Put yourself in the picture of this Scripture in your mind.

_____

_____

_____

_____

_____

From *Healing the Wounded Heart:* "I see and imagine the Lord Himself coming with a bucket and a mop, so to speak, to clean up the mess (our sin)."

Take time to pray, declaring to God what you have seen today.

Lord, today You said to me:

_____

_____

_____

_____

_____

_____

_____

_____

_____

(Please remember to enter a one-sentence synopsis in the Journal Summary section, which immediately follows the 49 daily meditations, and state what the Lord has spoken to you today.)

THE TRUTH BECOMES TRUE

What was the core Truth revealed to you through today's meditation?

_____

_____

_____

_____

_____

_____

Watch throughout the day to see where that Truth becomes personal truth to you and journal your thoughts on this page along with other significant Truths and impressions from your travels with the Lord today.

My HEALING JOURNEY

_____

_____

_____

_____

_____

_____

_____

_____

_____

Day 29

The Truth About Insecurity— "I Am Safe in the Arms of My Father"

Truth: I am surrounded by my Father.

Repeat this truth aloud. Close your eyes and rest a moment in this truth.

> *Just as Jerusalem is protected by mountains on every side, the Lord protects His people by holding them in His arms now and forever* (Psalm 125:2 CEV).

Meditate on this Scripture, saying it to yourself softly over and over again until you can say it with your eyes closed. As you repeat the Scripture, allow yourself to see it with the eyes of your heart. What is the picture you see in your mind's eye as you repeat the Scripture?

_____

_____

_____

What does the Scripture reveal about the heart of God?

_____

_____

_____

_____

What is the Lord speaking to you personally as you see the truth of this Scripture? Put yourself in the picture of this Scripture in your mind.

_____

_____

_____

_____

_____

From *Healing the Wounded Heart:* "The Scriptures are filled with promises of God's embracing presence for those who are secure in Him."

Take time to pray, declaring to God what you have seen today.

Lord, today You said to me:

_____

_____

_____

_____

_____

_____

_____

(Please remember to enter a one-sentence synopsis in the Journal Summary section, which immediately follows the 49 daily meditations, and state what the Lord has spoken to you today.)

THE TRUTH BECOMES TRUE

What was the core Truth revealed to you through today's meditation?

_____

_____

_____

_____

_____

Watch throughout the day to see where that Truth becomes personal truth to you and journal your thoughts on this page along with other significant Truths and impressions from your travels with the Lord today.

My HEALING JOURNEY

_____

_____

_____

_____

_____

_____

_____

_____

_____

DAY 30

THE TRUTH ABOUT INSECURITY— "I AM SAFE IN THE ARMS OF MY FATHER"

Truth: My Father holds me tenderly close to Him.

Repeat this truth aloud. Close your eyes and rest a moment in this truth.

He tends His flock like a shepherd: He gathers the lambs in His arms and carries them close to His heart... (Isaiah 40:11 NIV).

Meditate on this Scripture, saying it to yourself softly over and over again until you can say it with your eyes closed. As you repeat the Scripture, allow yourself to see it with the eyes of your heart. What is the picture you see in your mind's eye as you repeat the Scripture?

_____

_____

_____

_____

What does the Scripture reveal about the heart of God?

_____

_____

_____

_____

What is the Lord speaking to you personally as you see the truth of this Scripture? Put yourself in the picture of this Scripture in your mind.

_____

_____

_____

_____

_____

From *Healing the Wounded Heart:* "We live securely within God's embrace—an embrace from which no one can remove us."

Take time to pray, declaring to God what you have seen today.

Lord, today You said to me:

_____

_____

_____

_____

_____

_____

_____

_____

_____

(Please remember to enter a one-sentence synopsis in the Journal Summary section, which immediately follows the 49 daily meditations, and state what the Lord has spoken to you today.)

THE TRUTH BECOMES TRUE

What was the core Truth revealed to you through today's meditation?

_____

_____

_____

_____

_____

_____

Watch throughout the day to see where that Truth becomes personal truth to you and journal your thoughts on this page along with other significant Truths and impressions from your travels with the Lord today.

My HEALING JOURNEY

_____

_____

_____

_____

_____

_____

_____

_____

_____

_____

_____

DAY 31

THE TRUTH ABOUT INSECURITY— "I AM SAFE IN THE ARMS OF MY FATHER"

Truth: I am tucked away and safe.

Repeat this truth aloud. Close your eyes and rest a moment in this truth.

> *He will cover you with His feathers, and under His wings you will find refuge; His faithfulness will be your shield and rampart* (Psalm 91:4 NIV).

Meditate on this Scripture, saying it to yourself softly over and over again until you can say it with your eyes closed. As you repeat the Scripture, allow yourself to see it with the eyes of your heart. What is the picture you see in your mind's eye as you repeat the Scripture?

_____

_____

_____

What does the Scripture reveal about the heart of God?

_____

_____

_____

_____

What is the Lord speaking to you personally as you see the truth of this Scripture? Put yourself in the picture of this Scripture in your mind.

_____

_____

_____

_____

_____

From *Healing the Wounded Heart:* "We live securely within God's embrace—an embrace from which no one can remove us."

Take time to pray, declaring to God what you have seen today.

Lord, today You said to me:

_____

_____

_____

_____

_____

_____

_____

_____

_____

_____

(Please remember to enter a one-sentence synopsis in the Journal Summary section, which immediately follows the 49 daily meditations, and state what the Lord has spoken to you today.)

THE TRUTH BECOMES TRUE

What was the core Truth revealed to you through today's meditation?

_____

_____

_____

_____

_____

_____

Watch throughout the day to see where that Truth becomes personal truth to you and journal your thoughts on this page along with other significant Truths and impressions from your travels with the Lord today.

My HEALING JOURNEY

_____

_____

_____

_____

_____

_____

_____

_____

_____

_____

DAY 32

THE TRUTH ABOUT INSECURITY— "I AM SAFE IN THE ARMS OF MY FATHER"

Truth: I am hidden in my Father.

Repeat this truth aloud. Close your eyes and rest a moment in this truth.

> *For in the day of trouble He will keep me safe in His dwelling;*
> *He will hide me in the shelter of His tabernacle and set me high*
> *upon a rock* (Psalm 27:5 NIV).

Meditate on this Scripture, saying it to yourself softly over and over again until you can say it with your eyes closed. As you repeat the Scripture, allow yourself to see it with the eyes of your heart. What is the picture you see in your mind's eye as you repeat the Scripture?

_____

_____

_____

What does the Scripture reveal about the heart of God?

_____

_____

_____

_____

What is the Lord speaking to you personally as you see the truth of this Scripture? Put yourself in the picture of this Scripture in your mind.

_____

_____

_____

_____

_____

From *Healing the Wounded Heart:* "God is our refuge and our stronghold. He is our hiding place. We are safe in His grace that flows from His total security."

Take time to pray, declaring to God what you have seen today.

Lord, today You said to me:

_____

_____

_____

_____

_____

_____

_____

_____

(Please remember to enter a one-sentence synopsis in the Journal Summary section, which immediately follows the 49 daily meditations, and state what the Lord has spoken to you today.)

THE TRUTH BECOMES TRUE

What was the core Truth revealed to you through today's meditation?

_____

_____

_____

_____

_____

_____

Watch throughout the day to see where that Truth becomes personal truth to you and journal your thoughts on this page along with other significant Truths and impressions from your travels with the Lord today.

My HEALING JOURNEY

_____

_____

_____

_____

_____

_____

_____

_____

_____

_____

DAY 33

THE TRUTH ABOUT INSECURITY— "I AM SAFE IN THE ARMS OF MY FATHER"

Truth: My Father is with me regardless of what is happening around me. Repeat this truth aloud. Close your eyes and rest a moment in this truth.

> *When you pass through the waters, I will be with you; and when you pass through the rivers, they will not sweep over you. When you walk through the fire, you will not be burned; the flames will not set you ablaze* (Isaiah 43:2 NIV).

Meditate on this Scripture, saying it to yourself softly over and over again until you can say it with your eyes closed. As you repeat the Scripture, allow yourself to see it with the eyes of your heart. What is the picture you see in your mind's eye as you repeat the Scripture?

_____

_____

What does the Scripture reveal about the heart of God?

_____

_____

_____

_____

What is the Lord speaking to you personally as you see the truth of this Scripture? Put yourself in the picture of this Scripture in your mind.

_____

_____

_____

_____

_____

From *Healing the Wounded Heart:* "Even when the world around us seems threatening—indeed, when bad things happen—we are still safe in God and confident in His love for us."

Take time to pray, declaring to God what you have seen today.

Lord, today You said to me:

_____

_____

_____

_____

_____

_____

_____

(Please remember to enter a one-sentence synopsis in the Journal Summary section, which immediately follows the 49 daily meditations, and state what the Lord has spoken to you today.)

THE TRUTH BECOMES TRUE

What was the core Truth revealed to you through today's meditation?

_____

_____

_____

_____

_____

Watch throughout the day to see where that Truth becomes personal truth to you and journal your thoughts on this page along with other significant Truths and impressions from your travels with the Lord today.

My HEALING JOURNEY

_____

_____

_____

_____

_____

_____

_____

_____

_____

DAY 34

THE TRUTH ABOUT INSECURITY— "I AM SAFE IN THE ARMS OF MY FATHER"

Truth: My Father is continually available to help me.

Repeat this truth aloud. Close your eyes and rest a moment in this truth.

> *So we say with confidence, "The Lord is my helper; I will not be afraid. What can man do to me?"* (Hebrews 13:6 NIV)

Meditate on this Scripture, saying it to yourself softly over and over again until you can say it with your eyes closed. As you repeat the Scripture, allow yourself to see it with the eyes of your heart. What is the picture you see in your mind's eye as you repeat the Scripture?

_____

_____

_____

_____

What does the Scripture reveal about the heart of God?

_____

_____

_____

_____

What is the Lord speaking to you personally as you see the truth of this Scripture? Put yourself in the picture of this Scripture in your mind.

_____

_____

_____

_____

_____

From *Healing the Wounded Heart:* "The King relates to us solely on the basis of His own grace and provision. We are eternally secure at the table."

Take time to pray, declaring to God what you have seen today.

Lord, today You said to me:

_____

_____

_____

_____

_____

_____

_____

_____

(Please remember to enter a one-sentence synopsis in the Journal Summary section, which immediately follows the 49 daily meditations, and state what the Lord has spoken to you today.)

THE TRUTH BECOMES TRUE

What was the core Truth revealed to you through today's meditation?

_____

_____

_____

_____

_____

_____

Watch throughout the day to see where that Truth becomes personal truth to you and journal your thoughts on this page along with other significant Truths and impressions from your travels with the Lord today.

My HEALING JOURNEY

_____

_____

_____

_____

_____

_____

_____

_____

_____

DAY 35

THE TRUTH ABOUT INSECURITY— "I AM SAFE IN THE ARMS OF MY FATHER"

Truth: My Father is in control of my life.

Repeat this truth aloud. Close your eyes and rest a moment in this truth.

> *But I trust in You, O Lord; I say, "You are my God." My times are in Your hands; deliver me from my enemies and from those who pursue me* (Psalm 31:14-15 NIV).

Meditate on this Scripture, saying it to yourself softly over and over again until you can say it with your eyes closed. As you repeat the Scripture, allow yourself to see it with the eyes of your heart. What is the picture you see in your mind's eye as you repeat the Scripture?

_____

_____

_____

What does the Scripture reveal about the heart of God?

_____

_____

_____

_____

What is the Lord speaking to you personally as you see the truth of this Scripture? Put yourself in the picture of this Scripture in your mind.

_____

_____

_____

_____

_____

From *Healing the Wounded Heart:* "The truth is that the King knows where we are, and He woos us off the ledge to His table."

Take time to pray, declaring to God what you have seen today.

Lord, today You said to me:

_____

_____

_____

_____

_____

_____

_____

_____

_____

(Please remember to enter a one-sentence synopsis in the Journal Summary section, which immediately follows the 49 daily meditations, and state what the Lord has spoken to you today.)

THE TRUTH BECOMES TRUE

What was the core Truth revealed to you through today's meditation?

_____

_____

_____

_____

_____

_____

Watch throughout the day to see where that Truth becomes personal truth to you and journal your thoughts on this page along with other significant Truths and impressions from your travels with the Lord today.

My HEALING JOURNEY

_____

_____

_____

_____

_____

_____

_____

_____

_____

_____

DAY 36

THE TRUTH ABOUT DEFILEMENT— "THE FATHER HAS CLEANSED AND RESTORED ME"

Truth: My Father desires to restore me.

Repeat this truth aloud. Close your eyes and rest a moment in this truth.

And the God of all grace...will Himself restore you and make you strong, firm and steadfast (1 Peter 5:10 NIV).

Meditate on this Scripture, saying it to yourself softly over and over again until you can say it with your eyes closed. As you repeat the Scripture, allow yourself to see it with the eyes of your heart. What is the picture you see in your mind's eye as you repeat the Scripture?

_____

_____

What does the Scripture reveal about the heart of God?

_____

_____

_____

_____

What is the Lord speaking to you personally as you see the truth of this Scripture? Put yourself in the picture of this Scripture in your mind.

_____

_____

_____

_____

_____

From *Healing the Wounded Heart:* "God will restore us to all that we ever were intended to be in Him."

Take time to pray, declaring to God what you have seen today.

Lord, today You said to me:

_____

_____

_____

_____

_____

_____

_____

_____

_____

_____

(Please remember to enter a one-sentence synopsis in the Journal Summary section, which immediately follows the 49 daily meditations, and state what the Lord has spoken to you today.)

THE TRUTH BECOMES TRUE

What was the core Truth revealed to you through today's meditation?

_____

_____

_____

_____

_____

_____

Watch throughout the day to see where that Truth becomes personal truth to you and journal your thoughts on this page along with other significant Truths and impressions from your travels with the Lord today.

My HEALING JOURNEY

_____

_____

_____

_____

_____

_____

_____

_____

_____

_____

_____

DAY 37

THE TRUTH ABOUT DEFILEMENT—"THE FATHER HAS CLEANSED AND RESTORED ME"

Truth: Nothing that has happened is beyond the restoration of my Father.

Repeat this truth aloud. Close your eyes and rest a moment in this truth.

> *In all their distress He too was distressed, and the angel of His presence saved them. In His love and mercy He redeemed them; He lifted them up and carried them all the days of old* (Isaiah 63:9 NIV).

Meditate on this Scripture, saying it to yourself softly over and over again until you can say it with your eyes closed. As you repeat the Scripture, allow yourself to see it with the eyes of your heart. What is the picture you see in your mind's eye as you repeat the Scripture?

_____

_____

What does the Scripture reveal about the heart of God?

_____

_____

_____

_____

What is the Lord speaking to you personally as you see the truth of this Scripture? Put yourself in the picture of this Scripture in your mind.

_____

_____

_____

_____

_____

From *Healing the Wounded Heart:* "God always leads us back to His embrace and healing, even from the greatest wounding."

Take time to pray, declaring to God what you have seen today.

Lord, today You said to me:

_____

_____

_____

_____

_____

_____

_____

_____

_____

_____

(Please remember to enter a one-sentence synopsis in the Journal Summary section, which immediately follows the 49 daily meditations, and state what the Lord has spoken to you today.)

THE TRUTH BECOMES TRUE

What was the core Truth revealed to you through today's meditation?

_____

_____

_____

_____

_____

_____

Watch throughout the day to see where that Truth becomes personal truth to you and journal your thoughts on this page along with other significant Truths and impressions from your travels with the Lord today.

My HEALING JOURNEY

_____

_____

_____

_____

_____

_____

_____

_____

_____

_____

DAY 38

THE TRUTH ABOUT DEFILEMENT—"THE FATHER HAS CLEANSED AND RESTORED ME"

Truth: My Father can repair the damage that has been done.

Repeat this truth aloud. Close your eyes and rest a moment in this truth.

"For I will restore you to health and I will heal you of your wounds," declares the Lord... (Jeremiah 30:17).

Meditate on this Scripture, saying it to yourself softly over and over again until you can say it with your eyes closed. As you repeat the Scripture, allow yourself to see it with the eyes of your heart. What is the picture you see in your mind's eye as you repeat the Scripture?

_____

_____

_____

_____

What does the Scripture reveal about the heart of God?

_____

_____

_____

_____

What is the Lord speaking to you personally as you see the truth of this Scripture? Put yourself in the picture of this Scripture in your mind.

_____

_____

_____

_____

_____

From *Healing the Wounded Heart:* "As God heals us, we find a new life anchored in His healing presence and compassion."

Take time to pray, declaring to God what you have seen today.

Lord, today You said to me:

_____

_____

_____

_____

_____

_____

_____

_____

(Please remember to enter a one-sentence synopsis in the Journal Summary section, which immediately follows the 49 daily meditations, and state what the Lord has spoken to you today.)

THE TRUTH BECOMES TRUE

What was the core Truth revealed to you through today's meditation?

_____

_____

_____

_____

_____

_____

Watch throughout the day to see where that Truth becomes personal truth to you and journal your thoughts on this page along with other significant Truths and impressions from your travels with the Lord today.

My HEALING JOURNEY

_____

_____

_____

_____

_____

_____

_____

_____

_____

DAY 39

THE TRUTH ABOUT DEFILEMENT—"THE FATHER HAS CLEANSED AND RESTORED ME"

Truth: My Father is the God of fresh starts and renewal.

Repeat this truth aloud. Close your eyes and rest a moment in this truth.

> *Because of the Lord's great love we are not consumed, for His compassions never fail. They are new every morning; great is Your faithfulness* (Lamentations 3:22-23 NIV).

Meditate on this Scripture, saying it to yourself softly over and over again until you can say it with your eyes closed. As you repeat the Scripture, allow yourself to see it with the eyes of your heart. What is the picture you see in your mind's eye as you repeat the Scripture?

_____

_____

_____

What does the Scripture reveal about the heart of God?

_____

_____

_____

_____

What is the Lord speaking to you personally as you see the truth of this Scripture? Put yourself in the picture of this Scripture in your mind.

_____

_____

_____

_____

From *Healing the Wounded Heart:* "God desires to bring us back to Himself and into fruitful lives."

Take time to pray, declaring to God what you have seen today.

Lord, today You said to me:

_____

_____

_____

_____

_____

_____

_____

_____

(Please remember to enter a one-sentence synopsis in the Journal Summary section, which immediately follows the 49 daily meditations, and state what the Lord has spoken to you today.)

THE TRUTH BECOMES TRUE

What was the core Truth revealed to you through today's meditation?

_____

_____

_____

_____

_____

_____

Watch throughout the day to see where that Truth becomes personal truth to you and journal your thoughts on this page along with other significant Truths and impressions from your travels with the Lord today.

My HEALING JOURNEY

_____

_____

_____

_____

_____

_____

_____

_____

_____

_____

DAY 40

THE TRUTH ABOUT DEFILEMENT—"THE FATHER HAS CLEANSED AND RESTORED ME"

Truth: I have been made totally clean.

Repeat this truth aloud. Close your eyes and rest a moment in this truth.

> *Then I bathed you with water, washed off your blood from you and anointed you with oil* (Ezekiel 16:9).

Meditate on this Scripture, saying it to yourself softly over and over again until you can say it with your eyes closed. As you repeat the Scripture, allow yourself to see it with the eyes of your heart. What is the picture you see in your mind's eye as you repeat the Scripture?

_____

_____

_____

_____

What does the Scripture reveal about the heart of God?

_____

_____

_____

_____

What is the Lord speaking to you personally as you see the truth of this Scripture? Put yourself in the picture of this Scripture in your mind.

_____

_____

_____

_____

_____

From *Healing the Wounded Heart:* "God will restore us to all that we ever were intended to be in Him."

Take time to pray, declaring to God what you have seen today.

Lord, today You said to me:

_____

_____

_____

_____

_____

_____

_____

_____

_____

_____

(Please remember to enter a one-sentence synopsis in the Journal Summary section, which immediately follows the 49 daily meditations, and state what the Lord has spoken to you today.)

THE TRUTH BECOMES TRUE

What was the core Truth revealed to you through today's meditation?

_____

_____

_____

_____

_____

_____

Watch throughout the day to see where that Truth becomes personal truth to you and journal your thoughts on this page along with other significant Truths and impressions from your travels with the Lord today.

My HEALING JOURNEY

_____

_____

_____

_____

_____

_____

_____

_____

_____

_____

_____

DAY 41

THE TRUTH ABOUT DEFILEMENT—"THE FATHER HAS CLEANSED AND RESTORED ME"

Truth: I am chosen, treasured, and loved.

Repeat this truth aloud. Close your eyes and rest a moment in this truth.

Therefore, as God's chosen people, holy and dearly loved... (Colossians 3:12 NIV).

Meditate on this Scripture, saying it to yourself softly over and over again until you can say it with your eyes closed. As you repeat the Scripture, allow yourself to see it with the eyes of your heart. What is the picture you see in your mind's eye as you repeat the Scripture?

_____

_____

_____

_____

What does the Scripture reveal about the heart of God?

_____

_____

_____

_____

What is the Lord speaking to you personally as you see the truth of this Scripture? Put yourself in the picture of this Scripture in your mind.

_____

_____

_____

_____

_____

From *Healing the Wounded Heart:* "It is our relationship with Christ that distinguishes us from all others. It is our position in Christ that determines our worth and purpose."

Take time to pray, declaring to God what you have seen today.

Lord, today You said to me:

_____

_____

_____

_____

_____

_____

_____

_____

(Please remember to enter a one-sentence synopsis in the Journal Summary section, which immediately follows the 49 daily meditations, and state what the Lord has spoken to you today.)

THE TRUTH BECOMES TRUE

What was the core Truth revealed to you through today's meditation?

_____

_____

_____

_____

_____

_____

Watch throughout the day to see where that Truth becomes personal truth to you and journal your thoughts on this page along with other significant Truths and impressions from your travels with the Lord today.

My HEALING JOURNEY

_____

_____

_____

_____

_____

_____

_____

_____

_____

_____

DAY 42

THE TRUTH ABOUT DEFILEMENT—"THE FATHER HAS CLEANSED AND RESTORED ME"

Truth: I stand restored in the personal presence of God.

Repeat this truth aloud. Close your eyes and rest a moment in this truth.

O God, restore us and cause Your face to shine upon us, and we will be saved (Psalm 80:3).

Meditate on this Scripture, saying it to yourself softly over and over again until you can say it with your eyes closed. As you repeat the Scripture, allow yourself to see it with the eyes of your heart. What is the picture you see in your mind's eye as you repeat the Scripture?

_____

_____

_____

_____

What does the Scripture reveal about the heart of God?

_____

_____

_____

_____

What is the Lord speaking to you personally as you see the truth of this Scripture? Put yourself in the picture of this Scripture in your mind.

_____

_____

_____

_____

_____

From *Healing the Wounded Heart:* "God always leads us back to His embrace and healing, even from the greatest wounding."

Take time to pray, declaring to God what you have seen today.

Lord, today You said to me:

_____

_____

_____

_____

_____

_____

_____

_____

_____

(Please remember to enter a one-sentence synopsis in the Journal Summary section, which immediately follows the 49 daily meditations, and state what the Lord has spoken to you today.)

THE TRUTH BECOMES TRUE

What was the core Truth revealed to you through today's meditation?

_____

_____

_____

_____

_____

_____

Watch throughout the day to see where that Truth becomes personal truth to you and journal your thoughts on this page along with other significant Truths and impressions from your travels with the Lord today.

My HEALING JOURNEY

_____

_____

_____

_____

_____

_____

_____

_____

_____

_____

_____

Day 43

The Truth About Hopelessness— "I Have a Living Hope in Christ"

Truth: The Father's thoughts of me are always good and filled with hope. Repeat this truth aloud. Close your eyes and rest a moment in this truth.

> *"For I know the plans I have for you," declares the Lord, "plans to prosper you and not to harm you, plans to give you hope and a future"* (Jeremiah 29:11 NIV).

Meditate on this Scripture, saying it to yourself softly over and over again until you can say it with your eyes closed. As you repeat the Scripture, allow yourself to see it with the eyes of your heart. What is the picture you see in your mind's eye as you repeat the Scripture?

_____

_____

_____

What does the Scripture reveal about the heart of God?

_____

_____

_____

_____

What is the Lord speaking to you personally as you see the truth of this Scripture? Put yourself in the picture of this Scripture in your mind.

_____

_____

_____

_____

_____

From *Healing the Wounded Heart:* "The reality is that while things may seem hopeless according to our understanding, they are very much intact in God's view."

Take time to pray, declaring to God what you have seen today.

Lord, today You said to me:

_____

_____

_____

_____

_____

_____

_____

_____

(Please remember to enter a one-sentence synopsis in the Journal Summary section, which immediately follows the 49 daily meditations, and state what the Lord has spoken to you today.)

THE TRUTH BECOMES TRUE

What was the core Truth revealed to you through today's meditation?

_____

_____

_____

_____

_____

_____

Watch throughout the day to see where that Truth becomes personal truth to you and journal your thoughts on this page along with other significant Truths and impressions from your travels with the Lord today.

My HEALING JOURNEY

_____

_____

_____

_____

_____

_____

_____

_____

_____

_____

DAY 44

THE TRUTH ABOUT HOPELESSNESS— "I HAVE A LIVING HOPE IN CHRIST"

Truth: My Father is walking before me, preparing the way.

Repeat this truth aloud. Close your eyes and rest a moment in this truth.

> *Forget the former things; do not dwell on the past. See, I am*
> *doing a new thing! Now it springs up; do you not perceive it?*
> *I am making a way in the desert and streams in the wasteland*
> (Isaiah 43:18-19 NIV).

Meditate on this Scripture, saying it to yourself softly over and over again until you can say it with your eyes closed. As you repeat the Scripture, allow yourself to see it with the eyes of your heart. What is the picture you see in your mind's eye as you repeat the Scripture?

_____

_____

What does the Scripture reveal about the heart of God?

_____

_____

_____

_____

What is the Lord speaking to you personally as you see the truth of this Scripture? Put yourself in the picture of this Scripture in your mind.

_____

_____

_____

_____

_____

From *Healing the Wounded Heart:* "...while things may seem hopeless according to our understanding, they are very much intact in God's view."

Take time to pray, declaring to God what you have seen today.

Lord, today You said to me:

_____

_____

_____

_____

_____

_____

_____

_____

_____

(Please remember to enter a one-sentence synopsis in the Journal Summary section, which immediately follows the 49 daily meditations, and state what the Lord has spoken to you today.)

THE TRUTH BECOMES TRUE

What was the core Truth revealed to you through today's meditation?

_____

_____

_____

_____

_____

_____

Watch throughout the day to see where that Truth becomes personal truth to you and journal your thoughts on this page along with other significant Truths and impressions from your travels with the Lord today.

My HEALING JOURNEY

_____

_____

_____

_____

_____

_____

_____

_____

_____

_____

_____

DAY 45

THE TRUTH ABOUT HOPELESSNESS—
"I HAVE A LIVING HOPE IN CHRIST"

Truth: My Father's loving heart has planned help for me.

Repeat this truth aloud. Close your eyes and rest a moment in this truth.

> *The Lord will guide you always; He will satisfy your needs in a sun-scorched land and will strengthen your frame. You will be like a well-watered garden, like a spring whose waters never fail* (Isaiah 58:11 NIV).

Meditate on this Scripture, saying it to yourself softly over and over again until you can say it with your eyes closed. As you repeat the Scripture, allow yourself to see it with the eyes of your heart. What is the picture you see in your mind's eye as you repeat the Scripture?

_____

_____

What does the Scripture reveal about the heart of God?

_____

_____

_____

_____

What is the Lord speaking to you personally as you see the truth of this Scripture? Put yourself in the picture of this Scripture in your mind.

_____

_____

_____

_____

_____

From *Healing the Wounded Heart:* "Our hope is found in a greater revelation of Jesus Christ."

Take time to pray, declaring to God what you have seen today.

Lord, today You said to me:

_____

_____

_____

_____

_____

_____

_____

_____

_____

(Please remember to enter a one-sentence synopsis in the Journal Summary section, which immediately follows the 49 daily meditations, and state what the Lord has spoken to you today.)

THE TRUTH BECOMES TRUE

What was the core Truth revealed to you through today's meditation?

_____

_____

_____

_____

_____

Watch throughout the day to see where that Truth becomes personal truth to you and journal your thoughts on this page along with other significant Truths and impressions from your travels with the Lord today.

My HEALING JOURNEY

_____

_____

_____

_____

_____

_____

_____

_____

_____

DAY 46

THE TRUTH ABOUT HOPELESSNESS—
"I HAVE A LIVING HOPE IN CHRIST"

Truth: The Father is trustworthy in times of difficulty.

Repeat this truth aloud. Close your eyes and rest a moment in this truth.

Let him who walks in the dark, who has no light, trust in the name of the Lord and rely on his God (Isaiah 50:10 NIV).

Meditate on this Scripture, saying it to yourself softly over and over again until you can say it with your eyes closed. As you repeat the Scripture, allow yourself to see it with the eyes of your heart. What is the picture you see in your mind's eye as you repeat the Scripture?

_____

_____

_____

_____

What does the Scripture reveal about the heart of God?

_____

_____

_____

_____

What is the Lord speaking to you personally as you see the truth of this Scripture? Put yourself in the picture of this Scripture in your mind.

_____

_____

_____

_____

_____

From *Healing the Wounded Heart:* "Our hope is in the character of a good and faithful God, in a risen and powerful Lord."

Take time to pray, declaring to God what you have seen today.

Lord, today You said to me:

_____

_____

_____

_____

_____

_____

_____

_____

(Please remember to enter a one-sentence synopsis in the Journal Summary section, which immediately follows the 49 daily meditations, and state what the Lord has spoken to you today.)

THE TRUTH BECOMES TRUE

What was the core Truth revealed to you through today's meditation?

_____

_____

_____

_____

_____

_____

Watch throughout the day to see where that Truth becomes personal truth to you and journal your thoughts on this page along with other significant Truths and impressions from your travels with the Lord today.

My HEALING JOURNEY

_____

_____

_____

_____

_____

_____

_____

_____

_____

_____

_____

DAY 47

THE TRUTH ABOUT HOPELESSNESS— "I HAVE A LIVING HOPE IN CHRIST"

Truth: The Father makes a way for me, even through depression.

Repeat this truth aloud. Close your eyes and rest a moment in this truth.

You, O Lord, keep my lamp burning; my God turns my darkness into light (Psalm 18:28 NIV).

Meditate on this Scripture, saying it to yourself softly over and over again until you can say it with your eyes closed. As you repeat the Scripture, allow yourself to see it with the eyes of your heart. What is the picture you see in your mind's eye as you repeat the Scripture?

_____

_____

_____

_____

What does the Scripture reveal about the heart of God?

_____

_____

_____

_____

What is the Lord speaking to you personally as you see the truth of this Scripture? Put yourself in the picture of this Scripture in your mind.

_____

_____

_____

_____

_____

From *Healing the Wounded Heart:* "The character of God is the collateral of our hope."

Take time to pray, declaring to God what you have seen today.

Lord, today You said to me:

_____

_____

_____

_____

_____

_____

_____

_____

(Please remember to enter a one-sentence synopsis in the Journal Summary section, which immediately follows the 49 daily meditations, and state what the Lord has spoken to you today.)

THE TRUTH BECOMES TRUE

What was the core Truth revealed to you through today's meditation?

_____

_____

_____

_____

_____

Watch throughout the day to see where that Truth becomes personal truth to you and journal your thoughts on this page along with other significant Truths and impressions from your travels with the Lord today.

My HEALING JOURNEY

_____

_____

_____

_____

_____

_____

_____

_____

_____

_____

DAY 48

THE TRUTH ABOUT HOPELESSNESS— "I HAVE A LIVING HOPE IN CHRIST"

Truth: My Father is pouring out fresh mercy for me today.

Repeat this truth aloud. Close your eyes and rest a moment in this truth.

Weeping may last for the night, but a shout of joy comes in the morning (Psalm 30:5).

Meditate on this Scripture, saying it to yourself softly over and over again until you can say it with your eyes closed. As you repeat the Scripture, allow yourself to see it with the eyes of your heart. What is the picture you see in your mind's eye as you repeat the Scripture?

_____

_____

_____

_____

What does the Scripture reveal about the heart of God?

_____

_____

_____

_____

What is the Lord speaking to you personally as you see the truth of this Scripture?

Put yourself in the picture of this Scripture in your mind.

_____

_____

_____

_____

From *Healing the Wounded Heart:* "God is good. In eternity He will be glorified in our defeats and failures as much as or more than in our apparent triumphs."

Take time to pray, declaring to God what you have seen today.

Lord, today You said to me:

_____

_____

_____

_____

_____

_____

_____

_____

(Please remember to enter a one-sentence synopsis in the Journal Summary section, which immediately follows the 49 daily meditations, and state what the Lord has spoken to you today.)

THE TRUTH BECOMES TRUE

What was the core Truth revealed to you through today's meditation?

_____

_____

_____

_____

_____

_____

Watch throughout the day to see where that Truth becomes personal truth to you and journal your thoughts on this page along with other significant Truths and impressions from your travels with the Lord today.

My HEALING JOURNEY

_____

_____

_____

_____

_____

_____

_____

_____

_____

_____

DAY 49

THE TRUTH ABOUT HOPELESSNESS— "I HAVE A LIVING HOPE IN CHRIST"

Truth: I can do all things through Christ.

Repeat this truth aloud. Close your eyes and rest a moment in this truth.

I can do everything through Him who gives me strength (Philippians 4:13 NIV).

Meditate on this Scripture, saying it to yourself softly over and over again until you can say it with your eyes closed. As you repeat the Scripture, allow yourself to see it with the eyes of your heart. What is the picture you see in your mind's eye as you repeat the Scripture?

_____

_____

_____

_____

What does the Scripture reveal about the heart of God?

_____

_____

_____

_____

What is the Lord speaking to you personally as you see the truth of this Scripture? Put yourself in the picture of this Scripture in your mind.

_____

_____

_____

_____

_____

From *Healing the Wounded Heart:* "It is...our personal revelation of Jesus and the experiencing of His personal intimacy that heals us from hopelessness."

Take time to pray, declaring to God what you have seen today.

Lord, today You said to me:

_____

_____

_____

_____

_____

_____

_____

_____

_____

(Please remember to enter a one-sentence synopsis in the Journal Summary section, which immediately follows the 49 daily meditations, and state what the Lord has spoken to you today.)

THE TRUTH BECOMES TRUE

What was the core Truth revealed to you through today's meditation?

_____

_____

_____

_____

_____

_____

Watch throughout the day to see where that Truth becomes personal truth to you and journal your thoughts on this page along with other significant Truths and impressions from your travels with the Lord today.

My HEALING JOURNEY

_____

_____

_____

_____

_____

_____

_____

_____

_____

_____

JOURNAL SUMMARY

WEEK ONE JOURNAL SUMMARY

Summarizing what you have heard this week, write one sentence or phrase for each day on your healing journey.

Day 1

_____

_____

Day 2

_____

_____

Day 3

_____

_____

Day 4

_____

_____

Day 5

_____

_____

Day 6

_____

_____

Day 7

_____

_____

Now condense and summarize what you have learned this week about the Father's heart and what He has spoken to you.

_____

_____

_____

_____

_____

_____

_____

_____

_____

_____

_____

_____

_____

WEEK TWO JOURNAL SUMMARY

Summarizing what you have heard this week, write one sentence or phrase for each day on your healing journey.

Day 8

_____

_____

Day 9

_____

_____

Day 10

_____

_____

Day 11

_____

_____

Day 12

_____

_____

Day 13

_____

_____

Day 14

_____

_____

Now condense and summarize what you have learned this week about the Father's heart and what He has spoken to you.

_____

_____

_____

_____

_____

_____

_____

_____

_____

_____

_____

_____

WEEK THREE JOURNAL SUMMARY

Summarizing what you have heard this week, write one sentence or phrase for each day on your healing journey.

Day 15

_____

_____

Day 16

_____

_____

Day 17

_____

_____

Day 18

_____

_____

Day 19

_____

_____

Day 20

_____

_____

Day 21

_____

_____

Now condense and summarize what you have learned this week about the Father's heart and what He has spoken to you.

_____

_____

_____

_____

_____

_____

_____

_____

_____

_____

_____

_____

_____

WEEK FOUR JOURNAL SUMMARY

Summarizing what you have heard this week, write one sentence or phrase for each day on your healing journey.

Day 22

_____

_____

Day 23

_____

_____

Day 24

_____

_____

Day 25

_____

_____

Day 26

_____

_____

Day 27

_____

_____

Day 28

_____

_____

Now condense and summarize what you have learned this week about the Father's heart and what He has spoken to you.

_____

_____

_____

_____

_____

_____

_____

_____

_____

_____

_____

_____

WEEK FIVE JOURNAL SUMMARY

Summarizing what you have heard this week, write one sentence or phrase for each day on your healing journey.

Day 29

_____

_____

Day 30

_____

_____

Day 31

_____

_____

Day 32

_____

_____

Day 33

_____

_____

Day 34

_____

_____

Day 35

_____

_____

Now condense and summarize what you have learned this week about the Father's heart and what He has spoken to you.

_____

_____

_____

_____

_____

_____

_____

_____

_____

_____

_____

_____

_____

_____

_____

WEEK SIX JOURNAL SUMMARY

Summarizing what you have heard this week, write one sentence or phrase for each day on your healing journey.

Day 36

_____

_____

Day 37

_____

_____

Day 38

_____

_____

Day 39

_____

_____

Day 40

_____

_____

Day 41

_____

_____

Day 42

_____

_____

Now condense and summarize what you have learned this week about the Father's heart and what He has spoken to you.

_____

_____

_____

_____

_____

_____

_____

_____

_____

_____

_____

_____

WEEK SEVEN JOURNAL SUMMARY

Summarizing what you have heard this week, write one sentence or phrase for each day on your healing journey.

Day 43

_____

_____

Day 44

_____

_____

Day 45

_____

_____

Day 46

_____

_____

Day 47

_____

_____

Day 48

_____

_____

Day 49

_____

_____

Now condense and summarize what you have learned this week about the Father's heart and what He has spoken to you.

_____

_____

_____

_____

_____

_____

_____

_____

_____

_____

_____

_____

ADDITIONAL
HEALING SCRIPTURES BY TOPIC

We have included this section of the book for you to continue your healing journey. Here is a topical list of Scriptures to meditate upon as you did in the first section. We are providing several pages formatted as the first section, but with blanks for you to fill in a Scripture of your choice and topic from the list that follows or from any other topical reference, such as *Nave's Topical Bible* or any other source of your choosing. Simply write the verse in the blank line provided marked "My Daily Journey" and follow the instructions as you did in section one stating any images that come to mind, what they reveal about the heart of God and what they say to you personally.

Following is a list of additional healing Scriptures that you may use for further meditation. Simply follow the same pattern you have followed in the 49-day devotional. It is recommended that you establish journaling as a spiritual discipline for the rest of your spiritual walk. When the Lord speaks, write it down.

> *Record the vision and inscribe it on tablets, that the one who reads it may run* (Habakkuk 2:2).

Get in the habit of revisiting and summarizing what the Lord speaks to you; subsequently, your intimate knowledge of the Father's heart will grow.

Blessings to you,
Thom Gardner

Fear—You Are Not Alone.

Behold, I am with you and will keep you wherever you go, and will bring you back to this land; for I will not leave you until I have done what I have promised you (Genesis 28:15).

"Do not be afraid of them, for I am with you to deliver you," *declares the Lord* (Jeremiah 1:8).

Do not tremble and do not be afraid; have I not long since announced it to you and declared it? And you are My witnesses. Is there any God besides Me, or is there any other Rock? I know of none (Isaiah 44:8).

Be strong and courageous, do not be afraid or tremble at them, for the Lord your God is the one who goes with you. He will not fail you or forsake you (Deuteronomy 31:6).

Have I not commanded you? Be strong and courageous! Do not tremble or be dismayed, for the Lord your God is with you wherever you go (Joshua 1:9).

The Lord of hosts is with us; the God of Jacob is our stronghold (Psalm 46:7).

Be strong and courageous, do not fear or be dismayed because of the king of Assyria nor because of all the horde that is with him; for the one with us is greater than the one with him (2 Chronicles 32:7).

...Do not fear, for I have redeemed you; I have called you by name; you are Mine! When you pass through the waters, I will

be with you; and through the rivers, they will not overflow you. When you walk through the fire, you will not be scorched, nor will the flame burn you (Isaiah 43:1-2).

Rejection—You Are Accepted in Christ.

But we should always give thanks to God for you, brethren beloved by the Lord, because God has chosen you from the beginning for salvation through sanctification by the Spirit and faith in the truth (2 Thessalonians 2:13).

They will say of Me, "Only in the Lord are righteousness and strength." Men will come to Him, and all who were angry at Him will be put to shame. In the Lord all the offspring of Israel will be justified and will glory (Isaiah 45:24-25).

In His days Judah will be saved, and Israel will dwell securely; and this is His name by which He will be called, "The Lord our righteousness" (Jeremiah 23:6).

For all have sinned and fall short of the glory of God, being justified as a gift by His grace through the redemption which is in Christ Jesus (Romans 3:23-24).

For the kingdom of God is not eating and drinking, but righteousness and peace and joy in the Holy Spirit. For he who in this way serves Christ is acceptable to God and approved by men (Romans 14:17-18).

Having predestined us to adoption as sons by Jesus Christ to Himself, according to the good pleasure of His will, to the praise of the glory of His grace, by which He made us accepted in the Beloved (Ephesians 1:5-6 NKJV).

Worthlessness—You Are Approved in Christ, Handmade and Precious.

God created man in His own image, in the image of God He created him; male and female He created them (Genesis 1:27).

Know that the Lord Himself is God; it is He who has made us, and not we ourselves; we are His people and the sheep of His pasture (Psalm 100:3).

Your hands made me and fashioned me; give me understanding, that I may learn Your commandments (Psalm 119:73).

For You formed my inward parts; You wove me in my mother's womb. I will give thanks to You, for I am fearfully and wonderfully made; wonderful are Your works, and my soul knows it very well (Psalm 139:13-14).

The people whom I formed for Myself will declare My praise (Isaiah 43:21).

But by the grace of God I am what I am... (1 Corinthians 15:10).

Therefore if anyone is in Christ, he is a new creature; the old things passed away; behold, new things have come (2 Corinthians 5:17).

For we are His workmanship, created in Christ Jesus for good works, which God prepared beforehand so that we would walk in them (Ephesians 2:10).

Do not lie to one another, since you laid aside the old self with its evil practices, and have put on the new self who is being renewed to a true knowledge according to the image of the One who created him (Colossians 3:9-10).

Shame—You Are Clothed With Christ.

How blessed is he whose transgression is forgiven, whose sin is covered! (Psalm 32:1)

For all of you who were baptized into Christ have clothed yourselves with Christ (Galatians 3:27).

I will rejoice greatly in the Lord, my soul will exult in my God; for He has clothed me with garments of salvation, He has wrapped me with a robe of righteousness (Isaiah 61:10).

But put on the Lord Jesus Christ, and make no provision for the flesh in regard to its lusts (Romans 13:14).

Insecurity—You Are Safe in Christ.

The eternal God is a dwelling place, and underneath are the everlasting arms (Deuteronomy 33:27).

O Lord, how my adversaries have increased! Many are rising up against me. Many are saying of my soul, "There is no deliverance for him in God." Selah. But You, O Lord, are a shield about me, my glory, and the One who lifts my head (Psalm 3:1-3).

Many are the sorrows of the wicked, but he who trusts in the Lord, lovingkindness shall surround him (Psalm 32:10).

The angel of the Lord encamps around those who fear Him, and rescues them (Psalm 34:7).

The Lord is your keeper; the Lord is your shade on your right hand. The sun will not smite you by day, nor the moon by night. The Lord will protect you from all evil; He will keep your soul. The Lord will guard your going out and your coming in from this time forth and forever (Psalm 121:5-8).

Those who trust in the Lord are as Mount Zion, which cannot be moved but abides forever. As the mountains surround Jerusalem, so the Lord surrounds His people from this time forth and forever (Psalm 125:1-2).

My sheep hear My voice, and I know them, and they follow Me; and I give eternal life to them, and they will never perish; and no one will snatch them out of My hand. My Father, who has given them to Me, is greater than all; and no one is able to snatch them out of the Father's hand (John 10:27-29).

Defilement—You Are Restored in Christ.

O God, restore us and cause Your face to shine upon us, and we will be saved (Psalm 80:3).

"For I will restore you to health and I will heal you of your wounds," declares the Lord, "because they have called you an outcast, saying: 'It is Zion; no one cares for her'" (Jeremiah 30:17).

"Then I passed by you and saw you, and behold, you were at the time for love; so I spread My skirt over you and covered your nakedness. I also swore to you and entered into a covenant with you so that you became Mine," declares the Lord God (Ezekiel 16:8).

Also I will restore the captivity of My people Israel, and they will rebuild the ruined cities and live in them; they will also plant vineyards and drink their wine, and make gardens and eat their fruit (Amos 9:14).

For the Lord will restore the splendor of Jacob like the splendor of Israel, even though devastators have devastated them and destroyed their vine branches (Nahum 2:2).

Hopelessness—You Have a Living Hope in Christ.

O Israel, hope in the Lord; for with the Lord there is lovingkindness, and with Him is abundant redemption (Psalm 130:7).

For in hope we have been saved, but hope that is seen is not hope; for who hopes for what he already sees? But if we hope for what we do not see, with perseverance we wait eagerly for it (Romans 8:24-25).

Blessed be the God and Father of our Lord Jesus Christ, who according to His great mercy has caused us to be born again to a living hope through the resurrection of Jesus Christ from the dead, to obtain an inheritance which is imperishable and undefiled and will not fade away, reserved in heaven for you, who are protected by the power of God through faith for a salvation ready to be revealed in the last time (1 Peter 1:3-5).

Therefore, prepare your minds for action, keep sober in spirit, fix your hope completely on the grace to be brought to you at the revelation of Jesus Christ (1 Peter 1:13).

And everyone who has this hope fixed on Him purifies himself, just as He is pure (1 John 3:3).

PART III:

THE JOURNEY CONTINUES

"The Journey Continues"

INSTRUCTIONS

Your journey has begun and patterns of new life and intimacy with God are being established. By now, areas where your walk needs to be reinforced are becoming known to you so the journey will continue in such a way to allow you to focus on those individual areas of healing. As you continue on the journey, more freedom comes. Jesus said, *"If you continue in My word, then you are truly disciples of Mine; and you will know the truth, and the truth will make you free"* (John 8:31-32). As you continue to walk with Christ in this journey, more Truth breaks upon your life and you become more free.

By now you have established the practice in the 49 days of the journey. The journey now continues using additional Scripture texts that have been provided in the pages that follow. They are sorted according to the same seven core issues we focused for the first leg of the journey. Simply go to the topical list of Scriptures and select a verse each day and write that verse in the blank space under "My Daily Journey." Note that you may use any verse for this part of the journey, whether from this list of topical Scriptures or any other topical list, such as *The Thompson Chain Reference Bible* or *Nave's Topical Bible*. Follow the same pattern you did on the first part of the journey when we provided the daily verse for you. I suggest that you settle in a safe place with the Lord and ask Him for direction for the next verses. You may want to continue to meditate in one certain area—such as fear or rejection—or you may want to mix it up a bit. In either case, the Lord has a plan for you to seek after Him as you continue the journey.

The Lord bless you and reveal His deep love for you as you continue to walk together with Him through this next leg of the journey.

DAY 1

MY DAILY JOURNEY

Meditate on this Scripture, saying it to yourself softly over and over again until you can say it with your eyes closed. As you repeat the Scripture, allow yourself to see it with the eyes of your heart. What is the picture you see in your mind's eye as you repeat the Scripture?

_____

_____

What does the Scripture reveal about the heart of God?

_____

_____

What is the Lord speaking to you personally as you see the truth of this Scripture? Put yourself in the picture of this Scripture in your mind.

_____

_____

Take time to pray, declaring to God what you have seen today.

Lord, today You said to me:

_____

_____

_____

DAY 2

MY DAILY JOURNEY

Meditate on this Scripture, saying it to yourself softly over and over again until you can say it with your eyes closed. As you repeat the Scripture, allow yourself to see it with the eyes of your heart. What is the picture you see in your mind's eye as you repeat the Scripture?

_____

_____

What does the Scripture reveal about the heart of God?

_____

_____

What is the Lord speaking to you personally as you see the truth of this Scripture? Put yourself in the picture of this Scripture in your mind.

_____

_____

Take time to pray, declaring to God what you have seen today.

Lord, today You said to me:

_____

_____

_____

DAY 3

MY DAILY JOURNEY

Meditate on this Scripture, saying it to yourself softly over and over again until you can say it with your eyes closed. As you repeat the Scripture, allow yourself to see it with the eyes of your heart. What is the picture you see in your mind's eye as you repeat the Scripture?

_____

_____

What does the Scripture reveal about the heart of God?

_____

_____

What is the Lord speaking to you personally as you see the truth of this Scripture? Put yourself in the picture of this Scripture in your mind.

_____

_____

Take time to pray, declaring to God what you have seen today.

Lord, today You said to me:

_____

_____

_____

DAY 4

MY DAILY JOURNEY

Meditate on this Scripture, saying it to yourself softly over and over again until you can say it with your eyes closed. As you repeat the Scripture, allow yourself to see it with the eyes of your heart. What is the picture you see in your mind's eye as you repeat the Scripture?

_____

_____

What does the Scripture reveal about the heart of God?

_____

_____

What is the Lord speaking to you personally as you see the truth of this Scripture? Put yourself in the picture of this Scripture in your mind.

_____

_____

Take time to pray, declaring to God what you have seen today.

Lord, today You said to me:

_____

_____

_____

DAY 5

MY DAILY JOURNEY

Meditate on this Scripture, saying it to yourself softly over and over again until you can say it with your eyes closed. As you repeat the Scripture, allow yourself to see it with the eyes of your heart. What is the picture you see in your mind's eye as you repeat the Scripture?

_____

_____

What does the Scripture reveal about the heart of God?

_____

_____

What is the Lord speaking to you personally as you see the truth of this Scripture? Put yourself in the picture of this Scripture in your mind.

_____

_____

Take time to pray, declaring to God what you have seen today.
Lord, today You said to me:

_____

_____

_____

DAY 6

MY DAILY JOURNEY

Meditate on this Scripture, saying it to yourself softly over and over again until you can say it with your eyes closed. As you repeat the Scripture, allow yourself to see it with the eyes of your heart. What is the picture you see in your mind's eye as you repeat the Scripture?

_____

_____

What does the Scripture reveal about the heart of God?

_____

_____

What is the Lord speaking to you personally as you see the truth of this Scripture? Put yourself in the picture of this Scripture in your mind.

_____

_____

Take time to pray, declaring to God what you have seen today.

Lord, today You said to me:

_____

_____

DAY 7

MY DAILY JOURNEY

Meditate on this Scripture, saying it to yourself softly over and over again until you can say it with your eyes closed. As you repeat the Scripture, allow yourself to see it with the eyes of your heart. What is the picture you see in your mind's eye as you repeat the Scripture?

_____

_____

What does the Scripture reveal about the heart of God?

_____

_____

What is the Lord speaking to you personally as you see the truth of this Scripture? Put yourself in the picture of this Scripture in your mind.

_____

_____

Take time to pray, declaring to God what you have seen today.

Lord, today You said to me:

_____

_____

_____

DAY 8

MY DAILY JOURNEY

Meditate on this Scripture, saying it to yourself softly over and over again until you can say it with your eyes closed. As you repeat the Scripture, allow yourself to see it with the eyes of your heart. What is the picture you see in your mind's eye as you repeat the Scripture?

_____

_____

What does the Scripture reveal about the heart of God?

_____

_____

What is the Lord speaking to you personally as you see the truth of this Scripture? Put yourself in the picture of this Scripture in your mind.

_____

_____

Take time to pray, declaring to God what you have seen today.

Lord, today You said to me:

_____

_____

DAY 9

MY DAILY JOURNEY

Meditate on this Scripture, saying it to yourself softly over and over again until you can say it with your eyes closed. As you repeat the Scripture, allow yourself to see it with the eyes of your heart. What is the picture you see in your mind's eye as you repeat the Scripture?

_____

_____

What does the Scripture reveal about the heart of God?

_____

_____

What is the Lord speaking to you personally as you see the truth of this Scripture? Put yourself in the picture of this Scripture in your mind.

_____

_____

Take time to pray, declaring to God what you have seen today.

Lord, today You said to me:

_____

_____

_____

DAY 10

MY DAILY JOURNEY

Meditate on this Scripture, saying it to yourself softly over and over again until you can say it with your eyes closed. As you repeat the Scripture, allow yourself to see it with the eyes of your heart. What is the picture you see in your mind's eye as you repeat the Scripture?

_____

_____

What does the Scripture reveal about the heart of God?

_____

_____

What is the Lord speaking to you personally as you see the truth of this Scripture? Put yourself in the picture of this Scripture in your mind.

_____

_____

Take time to pray, declaring to God what you have seen today.

Lord, today You said to me:

_____

_____

_____

DAY 11

MY DAILY JOURNEY

Meditate on this Scripture, saying it to yourself softly over and over again until you can say it with your eyes closed. As you repeat the Scripture, allow yourself to see it with the eyes of your heart. What is the picture you see in your mind's eye as you repeat the Scripture?

_____

_____

What does the Scripture reveal about the heart of God?

_____

_____

What is the Lord speaking to you personally as you see the truth of this Scripture? Put yourself in the picture of this Scripture in your mind.

_____

_____

Take time to pray, declaring to God what you have seen today.

Lord, today You said to me:

_____

_____

_____

DAY 12

MY DAILY JOURNEY

Meditate on this Scripture, saying it to yourself softly over and over again until you can say it with your eyes closed. As you repeat the Scripture, allow yourself to see it with the eyes of your heart. What is the picture you see in your mind's eye as you repeat the Scripture?

_____

_____

What does the Scripture reveal about the heart of God?

_____

_____

What is the Lord speaking to you personally as you see the truth of this Scripture? Put yourself in the picture of this Scripture in your mind.

_____

_____

Take time to pray, declaring to God what you have seen today.

Lord, today You said to me:

_____

_____

_____

DAY 13

MY DAILY JOURNEY

Meditate on this Scripture, saying it to yourself softly over and over again until you can say it with your eyes closed. As you repeat the Scripture, allow yourself to see it with the eyes of your heart. What is the picture you see in your mind's eye as you repeat the Scripture?

_____

_____

What does the Scripture reveal about the heart of God?

_____

_____

What is the Lord speaking to you personally as you see the truth of this Scripture? Put yourself in the picture of this Scripture in your mind.

_____

_____

Take time to pray, declaring to God what you have seen today.
Lord, today You said to me:

_____

_____

_____

DAY 14

MY DAILY JOURNEY

Meditate on this Scripture, saying it to yourself softly over and over again until you can say it with your eyes closed. As you repeat the Scripture, allow yourself to see it with the eyes of your heart. What is the picture you see in your mind's eye as you repeat the Scripture?

_____

_____

What does the Scripture reveal about the heart of God?

_____

_____

What is the Lord speaking to you personally as you see the truth of this Scripture? Put yourself in the picture of this Scripture in your mind.

_____

_____

Take time to pray, declaring to God what you have seen today.

Lord, today You said to me:

_____

_____

_____

DAY 15

MY DAILY JOURNEY

Meditate on this Scripture, saying it to yourself softly over and over again until you can say it with your eyes closed. As you repeat the Scripture, allow yourself to see it with the eyes of your heart. What is the picture you see in your mind's eye as you repeat the Scripture?

_____

_____

What does the Scripture reveal about the heart of God?

_____

_____

What is the Lord speaking to you personally as you see the truth of this Scripture? Put yourself in the picture of this Scripture in your mind.

_____

_____

Take time to pray, declaring to God what you have seen today.
Lord, today You said to me:

_____

_____

_____

DAY 16

MY DAILY JOURNEY

Meditate on this Scripture, saying it to yourself softly over and over again until you can say it with your eyes closed. As you repeat the Scripture, allow yourself to see it with the eyes of your heart. What is the picture you see in your mind's eye as you repeat the Scripture?

_____

_____

What does the Scripture reveal about the heart of God?

_____

_____

What is the Lord speaking to you personally as you see the truth of this Scripture? Put yourself in the picture of this Scripture in your mind.

_____

_____

Take time to pray, declaring to God what you have seen today.

Lord, today You said to me:

_____

_____

_____

DAY 17

MY DAILY JOURNEY

Meditate on this Scripture, saying it to yourself softly over and over again until you can say it with your eyes closed. As you repeat the Scripture, allow yourself to see it with the eyes of your heart. What is the picture you see in your mind's eye as you repeat the Scripture?

_____

_____

What does the Scripture reveal about the heart of God?

_____

_____

What is the Lord speaking to you personally as you see the truth of this Scripture? Put yourself in the picture of this Scripture in your mind.

_____

_____

Take time to pray, declaring to God what you have seen today.
Lord, today You said to me:

_____

_____

_____

DAY 18

MY DAILY JOURNEY

Meditate on this Scripture, saying it to yourself softly over and over again until you can say it with your eyes closed. As you repeat the Scripture, allow yourself to see it with the eyes of your heart. What is the picture you see in your mind's eye as you repeat the Scripture?

_____

_____

What does the Scripture reveal about the heart of God?

_____

_____

What is the Lord speaking to you personally as you see the truth of this Scripture? Put yourself in the picture of this Scripture in your mind.

_____

_____

Take time to pray, declaring to God what you have seen today.

Lord, today You said to me:

_____

_____

_____

DAY 19

MY DAILY JOURNEY

Meditate on this Scripture, saying it to yourself softly over and over again until you can say it with your eyes closed. As you repeat the Scripture, allow yourself to see it with the eyes of your heart. What is the picture you see in your mind's eye as you repeat the Scripture?

_____

_____

What does the Scripture reveal about the heart of God?

_____

_____

What is the Lord speaking to you personally as you see the truth of this Scripture? Put yourself in the picture of this Scripture in your mind.

_____

_____

Take time to pray, declaring to God what you have seen today.
Lord, today You said to me:

_____

_____

_____

DAY 20

MY DAILY JOURNEY

Meditate on this Scripture, saying it to yourself softly over and over again until you can say it with your eyes closed. As you repeat the Scripture, allow yourself to see it with the eyes of your heart. What is the picture you see in your mind's eye as you repeat the Scripture?

_____

_____

What does the Scripture reveal about the heart of God?

_____

_____

What is the Lord speaking to you personally as you see the truth of this Scripture? Put yourself in the picture of this Scripture in your mind.

_____

_____

Take time to pray, declaring to God what you have seen today.

Lord, today You said to me:

_____

_____

_____

DAY 21

MY DAILY JOURNEY

Meditate on this Scripture, saying it to yourself softly over and over again until you can say it with your eyes closed. As you repeat the Scripture, allow yourself to see it with the eyes of your heart. What is the picture you see in your mind's eye as you repeat the Scripture?

_____

_____

What does the Scripture reveal about the heart of God?

_____

_____

What is the Lord speaking to you personally as you see the truth of this Scripture? Put yourself in the picture of this Scripture in your mind.

_____

_____

Take time to pray, declaring to God what you have seen today.
Lord, today You said to me:

_____

_____

_____

DAY 22

MY DAILY JOURNEY

Meditate on this Scripture, saying it to yourself softly over and over again until you can say it with your eyes closed. As you repeat the Scripture, allow yourself to see it with the eyes of your heart. What is the picture you see in your mind's eye as you repeat the Scripture?

_____

_____

What does the Scripture reveal about the heart of God?

_____

_____

What is the Lord speaking to you personally as you see the truth of this Scripture? Put yourself in the picture of this Scripture in your mind.

_____

_____

Take time to pray, declaring to God what you have seen today.

Lord, today You said to me:

_____

_____

_____

DAY 23

MY DAILY JOURNEY

Meditate on this Scripture, saying it to yourself softly over and over again until you can say it with your eyes closed. As you repeat the Scripture, allow yourself to see it with the eyes of your heart. What is the picture you see in your mind's eye as you repeat the Scripture?

_____

_____

What does the Scripture reveal about the heart of God?

_____

_____

What is the Lord speaking to you personally as you see the truth of this Scripture? Put yourself in the picture of this Scripture in your mind.

_____

_____

Take time to pray, declaring to God what you have seen today.

Lord, today You said to me:

_____

_____

_____

DAY 24

MY DAILY JOURNEY

Meditate on this Scripture, saying it to yourself softly over and over again until you can say it with your eyes closed. As you repeat the Scripture, allow yourself to see it with the eyes of your heart. What is the picture you see in your mind's eye as you repeat the Scripture?

_____

_____

What does the Scripture reveal about the heart of God?

_____

_____

What is the Lord speaking to you personally as you see the truth of this Scripture? Put yourself in the picture of this Scripture in your mind.

_____

_____

Take time to pray, declaring to God what you have seen today.

Lord, today You said to me:

_____

_____

_____

DAY 25

MY DAILY JOURNEY

Meditate on this Scripture, saying it to yourself softly over and over again until you can say it with your eyes closed. As you repeat the Scripture, allow yourself to see it with the eyes of your heart. What is the picture you see in your mind's eye as you repeat the Scripture?

_____

_____

What does the Scripture reveal about the heart of God?

_____

_____

What is the Lord speaking to you personally as you see the truth of this Scripture? Put yourself in the picture of this Scripture in your mind.

_____

_____

Take time to pray, declaring to God what you have seen today.

Lord, today You said to me:

_____

_____

_____

DAY 26

MY DAILY JOURNEY

Meditate on this Scripture, saying it to yourself softly over and over again until you can say it with your eyes closed. As you repeat the Scripture, allow yourself to see it with the eyes of your heart. What is the picture you see in your mind's eye as you repeat the Scripture?

_____

_____

What does the Scripture reveal about the heart of God?

_____

_____

What is the Lord speaking to you personally as you see the truth of this Scripture? Put yourself in the picture of this Scripture in your mind.

_____

_____

Take time to pray, declaring to God what you have seen today.

Lord, today You said to me:

_____

_____

_____

DAY 27

MY DAILY JOURNEY

Meditate on this Scripture, saying it to yourself softly over and over again until you can say it with your eyes closed. As you repeat the Scripture, allow yourself to see it with the eyes of your heart. What is the picture you see in your mind's eye as you repeat the Scripture?

_____

_____

What does the Scripture reveal about the heart of God?

_____

_____

What is the Lord speaking to you personally as you see the truth of this Scripture? Put yourself in the picture of this Scripture in your mind.

_____

_____

Take time to pray, declaring to God what you have seen today.

Lord, today You said to me:

_____

_____

_____

DAY 28

MY DAILY JOURNEY

Meditate on this Scripture, saying it to yourself softly over and over again until you can say it with your eyes closed. As you repeat the Scripture, allow yourself to see it with the eyes of your heart. What is the picture you see in your mind's eye as you repeat the Scripture?

_____

_____

What does the Scripture reveal about the heart of God?

_____

_____

What is the Lord speaking to you personally as you see the truth of this Scripture? Put yourself in the picture of this Scripture in your mind.

_____

_____

Take time to pray, declaring to God what you have seen today.

Lord, today You said to me:

_____

_____

_____

DAY 29

MY DAILY JOURNEY

Meditate on this Scripture, saying it to yourself softly over and over again until you can say it with your eyes closed. As you repeat the Scripture, allow yourself to see it with the eyes of your heart. What is the picture you see in your mind's eye as you repeat the Scripture?

_____

_____

What does the Scripture reveal about the heart of God?

_____

_____

What is the Lord speaking to you personally as you see the truth of this Scripture? Put yourself in the picture of this Scripture in your mind.

_____

_____

Take time to pray, declaring to God what you have seen today.

Lord, today You said to me:

_____

_____

_____

DAY 30

MY DAILY JOURNEY

Meditate on this Scripture, saying it to yourself softly over and over again until you can say it with your eyes closed. As you repeat the Scripture, allow yourself to see it with the eyes of your heart. What is the picture you see in your mind's eye as you repeat the Scripture?

_____

_____

What does the Scripture reveal about the heart of God?

_____

_____

What is the Lord speaking to you personally as you see the truth of this Scripture? Put yourself in the picture of this Scripture in your mind.

_____

_____

Take time to pray, declaring to God what you have seen today.

Lord, today You said to me:

_____

_____

_____

Day 31

My Daily Journey

Meditate on this Scripture, saying it to yourself softly over and over again until you can say it with your eyes closed. As you repeat the Scripture, allow yourself to see it with the eyes of your heart. What is the picture you see in your mind's eye as you repeat the Scripture?

_____

_____

What does the Scripture reveal about the heart of God?

_____

_____

What is the Lord speaking to you personally as you see the truth of this Scripture? Put yourself in the picture of this Scripture in your mind.

_____

_____

Take time to pray, declaring to God what you have seen today.
Lord, today You said to me:

_____

_____

_____

DAY 32

MY DAILY JOURNEY

Meditate on this Scripture, saying it to yourself softly over and over again until you can say it with your eyes closed. As you repeat the Scripture, allow yourself to see it with the eyes of your heart. What is the picture you see in your mind's eye as you repeat the Scripture?

_____

_____

What does the Scripture reveal about the heart of God?

_____

_____

What is the Lord speaking to you personally as you see the truth of this Scripture? Put yourself in the picture of this Scripture in your mind.

_____

_____

Take time to pray, declaring to God what you have seen today.

Lord, today You said to me:

_____

_____

_____

DAY 33

MY DAILY JOURNEY

Meditate on this Scripture, saying it to yourself softly over and over again until you can say it with your eyes closed. As you repeat the Scripture, allow yourself to see it with the eyes of your heart. What is the picture you see in your mind's eye as you repeat the Scripture?

_____

_____

What does the Scripture reveal about the heart of God?

_____

_____

What is the Lord speaking to you personally as you see the truth of this Scripture? Put yourself in the picture of this Scripture in your mind.

_____

_____

Take time to pray, declaring to God what you have seen today.
Lord, today You said to me:

_____

_____

_____

DAY 34

MY DAILY JOURNEY

Meditate on this Scripture, saying it to yourself softly over and over again until you can say it with your eyes closed. As you repeat the Scripture, allow yourself to see it with the eyes of your heart. What is the picture you see in your mind's eye as you repeat the Scripture?

_____

_____

What does the Scripture reveal about the heart of God?

_____

_____

What is the Lord speaking to you personally as you see the truth of this Scripture? Put yourself in the picture of this Scripture in your mind.

_____

_____

Take time to pray, declaring to God what you have seen today.

Lord, today You said to me:

_____

_____

_____

DAY 35

MY DAILY JOURNEY

Meditate on this Scripture, saying it to yourself softly over and over again until you can say it with your eyes closed. As you repeat the Scripture, allow yourself to see it with the eyes of your heart. What is the picture you see in your mind's eye as you repeat the Scripture?

_____

_____

What does the Scripture reveal about the heart of God?

_____

_____

What is the Lord speaking to you personally as you see the truth of this Scripture? Put yourself in the picture of this Scripture in your mind.

_____

_____

Take time to pray, declaring to God what you have seen today.
Lord, today You said to me:

_____

_____

_____

DAY 36

MY DAILY JOURNEY

Meditate on this Scripture, saying it to yourself softly over and over again until you can say it with your eyes closed. As you repeat the Scripture, allow yourself to see it with the eyes of your heart. What is the picture you see in your mind's eye as you repeat the Scripture?

_____

_____

What does the Scripture reveal about the heart of God?

_____

_____

What is the Lord speaking to you personally as you see the truth of this Scripture? Put yourself in the picture of this Scripture in your mind.

_____

_____

Take time to pray, declaring to God what you have seen today.

Lord, today You said to me:

_____

_____

_____

DAY 37

MY DAILY JOURNEY

Meditate on this Scripture, saying it to yourself softly over and over again until you can say it with your eyes closed. As you repeat the Scripture, allow yourself to see it with the eyes of your heart. What is the picture you see in your mind's eye as you repeat the Scripture?

_____

_____

What does the Scripture reveal about the heart of God?

_____

_____

What is the Lord speaking to you personally as you see the truth of this Scripture? Put yourself in the picture of this Scripture in your mind.

_____

_____

Take time to pray, declaring to God what you have seen today.
Lord, today You said to me:

_____

_____

_____

Day 38

MY DAILY JOURNEY

Meditate on this Scripture, saying it to yourself softly over and over again until you can say it with your eyes closed. As you repeat the Scripture, allow yourself to see it with the eyes of your heart. What is the picture you see in your mind's eye as you repeat the Scripture?

_____

_____

What does the Scripture reveal about the heart of God?

_____

_____

What is the Lord speaking to you personally as you see the truth of this Scripture? Put yourself in the picture of this Scripture in your mind.

_____

_____

Take time to pray, declaring to God what you have seen today.

Lord, today You said to me:

_____

_____

_____

Day 39

MY DAILY JOURNEY

Meditate on this Scripture, saying it to yourself softly over and over again until you can say it with your eyes closed. As you repeat the Scripture, allow yourself to see it with the eyes of your heart. What is the picture you see in your mind's eye as you repeat the Scripture?

_____

_____

What does the Scripture reveal about the heart of God?

_____

_____

What is the Lord speaking to you personally as you see the truth of this Scripture? Put yourself in the picture of this Scripture in your mind.

_____

_____

Take time to pray, declaring to God what you have seen today.
Lord, today You said to me:

_____

_____

_____

DAY 40

MY DAILY JOURNEY

Meditate on this Scripture, saying it to yourself softly over and over again until you can say it with your eyes closed. As you repeat the Scripture, allow yourself to see it with the eyes of your heart. What is the picture you see in your mind's eye as you repeat the Scripture?

_____

_____

What does the Scripture reveal about the heart of God?

_____

_____

What is the Lord speaking to you personally as you see the truth of this Scripture? Put yourself in the picture of this Scripture in your mind.

_____

_____

Take time to pray, declaring to God what you have seen today.

Lord, today You said to me:

_____

_____

_____

DAY 41

MY DAILY JOURNEY

Meditate on this Scripture, saying it to yourself softly over and over again until you can say it with your eyes closed. As you repeat the Scripture, allow yourself to see it with the eyes of your heart. What is the picture you see in your mind's eye as you repeat the Scripture?

_____

_____

What does the Scripture reveal about the heart of God?

_____

_____

What is the Lord speaking to you personally as you see the truth of this Scripture? Put yourself in the picture of this Scripture in your mind.

_____

_____

Take time to pray, declaring to God what you have seen today.
Lord, today You said to me:

_____

_____

_____

DAY 42

MY DAILY JOURNEY

Meditate on this Scripture, saying it to yourself softly over and over again until you can say it with your eyes closed. As you repeat the Scripture, allow yourself to see it with the eyes of your heart. What is the picture you see in your mind's eye as you repeat the Scripture?

_____

_____

What does the Scripture reveal about the heart of God?

_____

_____

What is the Lord speaking to you personally as you see the truth of this Scripture? Put yourself in the picture of this Scripture in your mind.

_____

_____

Take time to pray, declaring to God what you have seen today.

Lord, today You said to me:

_____

_____

_____

DAY 43

MY DAILY JOURNEY

Meditate on this Scripture, saying it to yourself softly over and over again until you can say it with your eyes closed. As you repeat the Scripture, allow yourself to see it with the eyes of your heart. What is the picture you see in your mind's eye as you repeat the Scripture?

_____

_____

What does the Scripture reveal about the heart of God?

_____

_____

What is the Lord speaking to you personally as you see the truth of this Scripture? Put yourself in the picture of this Scripture in your mind.

_____

_____

Take time to pray, declaring to God what you have seen today.
Lord, today You said to me:

_____

_____

_____

DAY 44

MY DAILY JOURNEY

Meditate on this Scripture, saying it to yourself softly over and over again until you can say it with your eyes closed. As you repeat the Scripture, allow yourself to see it with the eyes of your heart. What is the picture you see in your mind's eye as you repeat the Scripture?

_____

_____

What does the Scripture reveal about the heart of God?

_____

_____

What is the Lord speaking to you personally as you see the truth of this Scripture? Put yourself in the picture of this Scripture in your mind.

_____

_____

Take time to pray, declaring to God what you have seen today.

Lord, today You said to me:

_____

_____

_____

DAY 45

MY DAILY JOURNEY

Meditate on this Scripture, saying it to yourself softly over and over again until you can say it with your eyes closed. As you repeat the Scripture, allow yourself to see it with the eyes of your heart. What is the picture you see in your mind's eye as you repeat the Scripture?

_____

_____

What does the Scripture reveal about the heart of God?

_____

_____

What is the Lord speaking to you personally as you see the truth of this Scripture? Put yourself in the picture of this Scripture in your mind.

_____

_____

Take time to pray, declaring to God what you have seen today.

Lord, today You said to me:

_____

_____

_____

DAY 46

MY DAILY JOURNEY

Meditate on this Scripture, saying it to yourself softly over and over again until you can say it with your eyes closed. As you repeat the Scripture, allow yourself to see it with the eyes of your heart. What is the picture you see in your mind's eye as you repeat the Scripture?

_____

_____

What does the Scripture reveal about the heart of God?

_____

_____

What is the Lord speaking to you personally as you see the truth of this Scripture? Put yourself in the picture of this Scripture in your mind.

_____

_____

Take time to pray, declaring to God what you have seen today.

Lord, today You said to me:

_____

_____

_____

DAY 47

MY DAILY JOURNEY

Meditate on this Scripture, saying it to yourself softly over and over again until you can say it with your eyes closed. As you repeat the Scripture, allow yourself to see it with the eyes of your heart. What is the picture you see in your mind's eye as you repeat the Scripture?

_____

_____

What does the Scripture reveal about the heart of God?

_____

_____

What is the Lord speaking to you personally as you see the truth of this Scripture? Put yourself in the picture of this Scripture in your mind.

_____

_____

Take time to pray, declaring to God what you have seen today.
Lord, today You said to me:

_____

_____

_____

DAY 48

MY DAILY JOURNEY

Meditate on this Scripture, saying it to yourself softly over and over again until you can say it with your eyes closed. As you repeat the Scripture, allow yourself to see it with the eyes of your heart. What is the picture you see in your mind's eye as you repeat the Scripture?

_____

_____

What does the Scripture reveal about the heart of God?

_____

_____

What is the Lord speaking to you personally as you see the truth of this Scripture? Put yourself in the picture of this Scripture in your mind.

_____

_____

Take time to pray, declaring to God what you have seen today.

Lord, today You said to me:

_____

_____

_____

DAY 49

MY DAILY JOURNEY

Meditate on this Scripture, saying it to yourself softly over and over again until you can say it with your eyes closed. As you repeat the Scripture, allow yourself to see it with the eyes of your heart. What is the picture you see in your mind's eye as you repeat the Scripture?

_____

_____

What does the Scripture reveal about the heart of God?

_____

_____

What is the Lord speaking to you personally as you see the truth of this Scripture? Put yourself in the picture of this Scripture in your mind.

_____

_____

Take time to pray, declaring to God what you have seen today.
Lord, today You said to me:

_____

_____

_____

PART IV:

MY ANXIOUS THOUGHTS

"MY ANXIOUS THOUGHTS"

INSTRUCTIONS

*We use our powerful God-tools for smashing warped philoso-
phies, tearing down barriers erected against the truth of God,
fitting every loose thought and emotion and impulse into the
structure of life shaped by Christ* (2 Corinthians 10:5 TM).

As you continue on the Healing Journey, there will be days and thoughts
that arise out of daily life that don't agree with the new person you are
becoming in this healing season of your life. When those stray thoughts arise,
we need to know where they came from and tell them the truth.

I love the way The Message puts the Scripture listed above, that as we continue in the Truth of God's Word we are *"fitting every loose thought and emotion and impulse into the structure of life shaped by Christ."* To be sure, we will
experience thoughts and emotions that are "loose"—out of control. We take
those thoughts and emotions captive. If what we are thinking and feeling do
not agree with the heart of Christ, then there is healing available for us. We
simply take those thoughts and feelings and compare them with what Jesus
says.

The pages ahead follow a format that will allow you to shape your thoughts
according to the Truth of God's Word and the presence of Christ. Beloved,
there is no place of darkness where you are separated from the Spirit of God—
nowhere beyond His loving reach.

The instructions are simple: When an anxious thought arises along the way of your life's journey, simply write it down in the spaces labeled, "What Happened?" On the next lines write how you reacted to what happened where it says, "What Did I Feel and Why?" Now quiet your heart and get into a safe place and ask the Lord, "What Is the Truth?" (Please refer to the instructions on the safe place in the chapter called "Safe to Heal.")

Here is an example:

I was in the grocery store and ran into a friend of mine who asked me if I was going to attend a gathering at a neighbor's house. In fact, I didn't know about the gathering and suddenly felt angry and a little rejected. I asked myself, "What's wrong with me that I was not invited?"

When I returned home I sat down for a moment and gathered up my loose thoughts and emotions.

WHAT HAPPENED?

I was at the store when I heard about a gathering I was not invited to.

WHAT DID I FEEL AND WHY?

I felt rejected and asked myself what was wrong with me.

WHAT IS THE TRUTH?

Now I quieted myself in the safe place with Jesus as I meditated on Psalm 23 finding myself being led by still waters. I simply asked the Shepherd, "Lord, what is the Truth about my not being invited to my neighbor's gathering? Is there something wrong with me?"

Now I listened to my heart in the presence of the Lord and felt Him saying these words to me.

"Son, they may have forgotten or assumed that you already knew about the gathering. Your life and value does not depend upon an invitation to the party. You belong to Me!"

THE WHOLE TRUTH

While I felt rejected and unworthy not being invited to the gathering, the Truth is that it may have been an oversight.

MORE TRUTH

It is a healthy thing to get into the habit of gathering up those loose thoughts that fly through our heads and hearts. We don't have to be in a place to write things out in this fashion. Eventually this can become a way of living. There are several pages that follow in this anxious thought journal, but you can use this pattern in any journal or notebook to gather up loose thoughts.

May the Lord bless and teach you His Truth and make your heart like His.

My Anxious Thoughts Journal

WHAT HAPPENED?

_____

_____

WHAT DID I FEEL AND WHY?

_____

_____

WHAT IS THE TRUTH?

_____

_____

THE WHOLE TRUTH

_____

_____

MORE TRUTH

_____

_____

_____

WHAT HAPPENED?

_____

_____

WHAT DID I FEEL AND WHY?

_____

_____

_____

WHAT IS THE TRUTH?

_____

_____

_____

THE WHOLE TRUTH

_____

_____

_____

MORE TRUTH

_____

_____

_____

WHAT HAPPENED?

_____

_____

WHAT DID I FEEL AND WHY?

_____

_____

_____

WHAT IS THE TRUTH?

_____

_____

_____

THE WHOLE TRUTH

_____

_____

_____

MORE TRUTH

_____

_____

_____

WHAT HAPPENED?

_____

_____

WHAT DID I FEEL AND WHY?

_____

_____

_____

WHAT IS THE TRUTH?

_____

_____

_____

THE WHOLE TRUTH

_____

_____

_____

MORE TRUTH

_____

_____

_____

WHAT HAPPENED?

_____

_____

WHAT DID I FEEL AND WHY?

_____

_____

_____

WHAT IS THE TRUTH?

_____

_____

_____

THE WHOLE TRUTH

_____

_____

_____

MORE TRUTH

_____

_____

_____

YOU CAN HEAR GOD'S VOICE!

Used by permission of Dr. Mark Virkler[1]

The age in which we live is so married to rationalism and cognitive, analytical thought that we almost mock when we hear of one actually claiming to be able to hear the voice of God. However, we do not scoff, for several reasons. First, men and women throughout the Bible heard God's voice. Also, there are some highly effective and reputable men and women of God alive today who demonstrate that they hear God's voice. Finally, there is a deep hunger within us all to commune with God, and hear Him speak within our hearts.

As a born-again, Bible-believing Christian, I struggled unsuccessfully for years to hear God's voice. I prayed, fasted, studied my Bible and listened for a voice within, all to no avail. There was no inner voice that I could hear! Then God set me aside for a year to study, read, and experiment in the area of learning to hear His voice. During that time, the Lord taught me four keys that opened the door to two-way prayer. I have discovered that not only do they work for me, but they have worked for many thousands of believers who have been taught to use them, bringing tremendous intimacy to their Christian experience and transforming their very way of living. This will happen to you also as you seek God, utilizing the following four keys. They are all found in Habakkuk 2:1-2. I encourage you to read this passage before going on.

Key #1—God's voice in our hearts sounds like a flow of spontaneous thoughts. Therefore, when I tune to God, I tune to spontaneity. The Bible says that *"the Lord answered me and said..."* (Hab. 2:2). Habakkuk knew the sound of God's voice. Elijah described it as a *"still small voice"* (1 Kings 19:12 NKJV).

I had always listened for an inner audible voice, and surely God can and does speak that way at times. However, I have found that for most of us, most of the time, God's inner voice comes to us as spontaneous thoughts, visions, feelings, or impressions. For example, haven't each of us had the experience of driving down the road and having a thought come to us to pray for a certain person? We generally acknowledge this to be the voice of God calling us to pray for that individual.

My question to you is, "What did God's voice sound like as you drove in your car? Was it an inner, audible voice, or was it a spontaneous thought that lit upon your mind?" Most of you would say that God's voice came to you as a spontaneous thought.

So I thought to myself, "Maybe when I listen for God's voice, I should be listening for a flow of spontaneous thoughts. Maybe spirit-level communication is received as spontaneous thoughts, impressions, feelings, and visions." Through experimentation and feedback from thousands of others, I am now convinced that this is so.

The Bible confirms this in many ways. The definition of *paga*, the Hebrew word for intercession, is "a chance encounter or an accidental intersecting." When God lays people on our hearts for intercession, He does it through *paga,* a chance encounter thought, accidentally intersecting our thought processes. Therefore, when I tune to God, I tune to chance-encounter thoughts or spontaneous thoughts. When I am poised quietly before God in prayer, I have found that the flow of spontaneous thoughts that comes is quite definitely from God.

Key #2—I must learn to still my own thoughts and emotions, so that I can sense God's flow of thoughts and emotions within me. Habakkuk said, *"I will stand on my guard post and station myself on the rampart..."* (Hab. 2:1). Habakkuk knew that in order to hear God's quiet, inner, spontaneous thoughts, he had to first go to a quiet place and still his own thoughts and emotions. Psalm 46:10 encourages us to be still, and know that He is God. There is a deep inner knowing (spontaneous flow) in our spirits that each of us can experience when we quiet our flesh and our minds.

I have found several simple ways to quiet myself so that I can more readily pick up God's spontaneous flow. Loving God through a quiet worship song is a most effective means for me (see 2 Kings 3:15). It is as I become still (thoughts, will, and emotions) and am poised before God that the divine flow is realized.

Therefore, after I worship quietly and then become still, I open myself for that spontaneous flow. If thoughts come to me of things I have forgotten to do, I write them down and then dismiss them. If thoughts of guilt or unworthiness come to my mind, I repent thoroughly, receive the washing of the blood of the Lamb, and put on His robe of righteousness, seeing myself spotless before the presence of God (see Isa. 61:10; Col. 1:22).

As I fix my gaze upon Jesus (see Heb. 12:2), becoming quiet in His presence, and sharing with Him what is on my heart, I find that two-way dialogue begins to flow. Spontaneous thoughts flow from the throne of God to me, and I find that I am actually conversing with the King of Kings. It is very important that you become still and properly focused if you are going to receive the pure word of God. If you are not still, you will simply be receiving your own thoughts. If you are not properly focused on Jesus, you will receive an impure flow, because the intuitive flow comes out of that upon which you have fixed your eyes. Therefore, if you fix your eyes upon Jesus, the intuitive flow comes from Jesus. If you fix your gaze upon some desire of your heart, the intuitive flow comes out of that desire of your heart. To have a pure flow you must first of all become still, and secondly, you must carefully fix your eyes upon Jesus. Again I will say, quietly worshiping the King, and then receiving out of the stillness that follows quite easily accomplish this.

Key #3—As I pray, I fix the eyes of my heart upon Jesus, seeing in the Spirit the dreams and visions of Almighty God. We have already alluded to this principle in the previous paragraphs; however, we need to develop it a bit further. Habakkuk said, *"I will keep watch to see,"* and God said, *"Record the vision"* (Hab. 2:1-2). It is very interesting that Habakkuk was going to actually start looking for vision as he prayed. He was going to open the eyes of his heart, and look into the spirit world to see what God wanted to show him. This is an intriguing idea.

I had never thought of opening the eyes of my heart and looking for vision. However, the more I thought of it, the more I realized this was exactly what God intends for me to do. He gave me eyes in my heart. They are to be used to see in the spirit world the vision and movement of Almighty God. I believe there is an active spirit world functioning all around me. This world is full of angels, demons, the Holy Spirit, the omnipresent God, and His omnipresent Son, Jesus. There is no reason for me not to see it, other than my rational culture, which tells me not to believe it is even there and provides no instruction on how to become open to seeing this spirit world.

The most obvious prerequisite to seeing is that we need to look. Daniel was seeing a vision in his mind and he said, *"I was looking...I kept looking...I kept looking"* (Dan. 7:2,9,13). Now as I pray, I look for Jesus present with me, and I watch Him as He speaks to me, doing and saying the things that are on His heart. Many Christians will find that if they will only look, they will see. Jesus is Immanuel, *"God with us"* (Matt. 1:23). It is as simple as that. You will see a spontaneous inner vision in a manner similar to receiving spontaneous inner thoughts.

You can see Christ present with you in a comfortable setting, because Christ is present with you in a comfortable setting. Actually, you will probably discover that inner vision comes so easily you will have a tendency to reject it, thinking that it is just you. (Doubt is satan's most effective weapon against the Church.) However, if you will persist in recording these visions, your doubt will soon be overcome by faith as you recognize that the content of them could only be birthed in Almighty God.

God continually revealed Himself to His covenant people using dream and vision. He did so from Genesis to Revelation and said that, since the Holy Spirit was poured out in Acts 2, we should expect to receive a continuing flow of dreams and visions (see Acts 2:1-4,17). Jesus, our perfect Example, demonstrated this ability of living out of ongoing contact with Almighty God. He said that He did nothing on His own initiative, but only that which He saw the Father doing, and heard the Father saying (see John 5:19-20,30). What an incredible way to live!

Is it actually possible for us to live out of the divine initiative as Jesus did? A major purpose of Jesus' death and resurrection was that the veil be torn from top to bottom, giving us access into the immediate presence of God, and we are commanded to draw near (see Luke 23:45; Heb. 10:19-22). Therefore, even though what I am describing seems a bit unusual to a rational twentieth-century culture, it is demonstrated and described as being a central biblical teaching and experience. It is time to restore to the Church all that belongs to the Church.

Because of their intensely rational nature and existence in an overly rational culture, some will need more assistance and understanding of these truths before they can move into them. They will find this help in the book *Communion With God* by the same authors.

Key #4—Journaling, the writing out of our prayers and God's answers, provides a great new freedom in hearing God's voice. God told Habakkuk to *"record the vision and inscribe it on tablets..."* (Hab. 2:2). It had never crossed my mind to write out my prayers and God's answers as Habakkuk did at God's command. If you begin to search Scripture for this idea, you will find hundreds of chapters demonstrating it (Psalms, many of the prophets, Revelation). Why then hadn't I ever thought of it? I called the process "journaling," and I began experimenting with it. I discovered it to be a fabulous facilitator to clearly discerning God's inner, spontaneous flow, because as I journaled I was able to write in faith for long periods of time, simply believing it was God. I did not have to test it as I was receiving it (which jams one's receiver), because I knew that when the flow was over I could go back and test and examine it carefully, making sure that it lined up with Scripture.

You will be amazed when you attempt journaling. Doubt may hinder you at first, but throw it off, reminding yourself that it is a biblical concept, and that God is present, speaking to His children. Don't take yourself too seriously. When you do, you become tense and get in the way of the Holy Spirit's movement. It is when we cease our labors and enter His rest that God is free to flow (see Heb. 4:10). Therefore, put a smile on your face, sit back comfortably, get out your pen and paper, and turn your attention toward God in praise and worship, seeking His face. As you write out your question to God and become still, fixing your gaze on Jesus, Who is present with you, you will suddenly have a very good thought in response to your question. Don't doubt it, simply write it down. Later, as you read your journaling, you, too, will be blessed to discover that you are indeed dialoguing with God.

Some final notes: No one should attempt this without having first read through at least the New Testament (preferably, the entire Bible), nor should one attempt this unless he is submitted to solid, spiritual leadership. All major directional moves that come through journaling should be submitted before being acted upon.

ENDNOTE

1. For a complete teaching on this topic, order the *Communion With God Study Guide* at www.CWGministries.org or call 716-652-6990. An online catalog of 50 books is available by Mark and Patti Virkler, as well as 100 college courses through external degree. For more information, you can send an e-mail to: cwg@cwgministries.org.

MORE ABOUT THOM GARDNER AND HIS MINISTRY

The mission of Grace and Truth Fellowship, Inc., is to transform local churches into healing centers. Serving as president of this ministry, Thom Gardner is available as a speaker/teacher for seminars, conferences, or other extended meetings. Grace and Truth Fellowship, Inc., also offers the Healing the Wounded Heart Training Seminar to equip the local church to bring healing to wounded hearts. The purpose of the seminar is to help participants find personal freedom through confrontation of their own past wounds, and then equip them to bring healing to others.

Healing the Wounded Heart Training Seminar is a three-day seminar that covers the material in this book and offers instruction and practice in the facilitation of this approach to healing wounded hearts. Our goal is to multiply, rather than monopolize, this approach to the ministry of inner healing.

If you are interested in attending a Healing the Wounded Heart Training Seminar, contact Grace and Truth Fellowship, Inc., at 717-263-6869, or see our Web site at www.graceandtruthfellowship.com.

ANOTHER BOOK BY THOM GARDNER

Turned Toward Mercy